Charles Hutchinson Gabriel, Isaac Naylor

Songs of the Pentecost for the forward Gospel Movement

Charles Hutchinson Gabriel, Isaac Naylor

Songs of the Pentecost for the forward Gospel Movement

ISBN/EAN: 9783337372507

Printed in Europe, USA, Canada, Australia, Japan

Cover: Foto ©Lupo / pixelio.de

More available books at **www.hansebooks.com**

No. 2. BE A GOLDEN SUNBEAM.

Isaac Naylor. Chas. H. Gabriel.
Companion to "Scatter Sunshine." No. 115.

1. Be a gold-en sun-beam, ra-di-ant and bright, Chasing from life's path-way sor-row's frowning night; With thy gold-en sun-light dry the dew-y tear, Scat-ter from the sad heart all its doubt and fear.
2. When the way is gloom-y, cheer it with a song,— Ban-ish mist and shad-ow as you march a-long; In the place of bri-ars, strew the fairest flow'rs, Wreathing brows with roses pluck'd from heav'nly bow'rs.
3. Be a gold-en sun-beam, bright, and pure, and fair; With thy smiles and son-nets light-en hu-man care; With the sweet-est mu-sic from the harp of love, Lure the sad and wea-ry to our home a-bove.

CHORUS.

{ Be a gold-en sun-beam, beau-ti-ful and bright, Scat-ter-ing clouds and darkness with thy shining light:
  Be a gold-en sun-beam, joy-ful-ly and glad, Scat-ter-ing rays of sun-light when the way is sad.

COPYRIGHT, 1894, BY CHAS. H. GABRIEL.

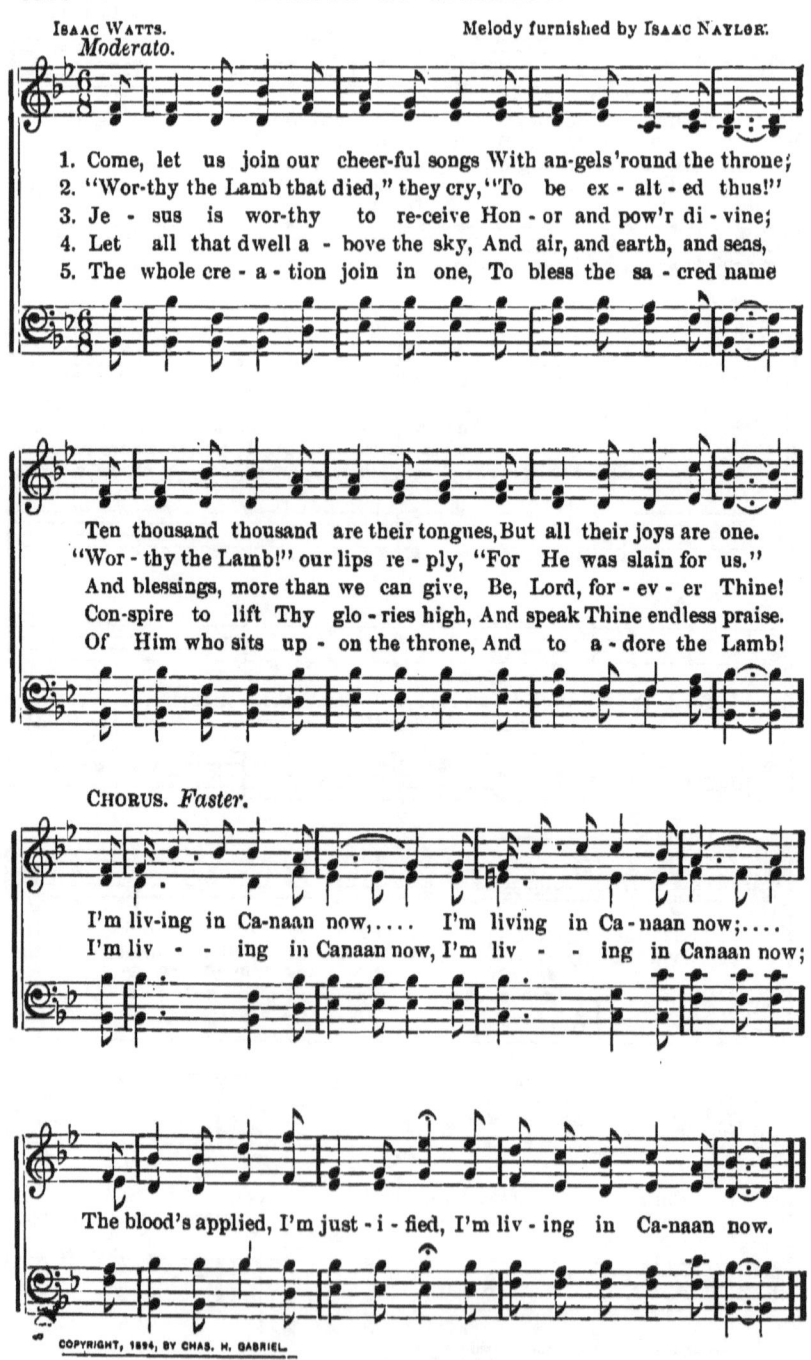

Look and Live.

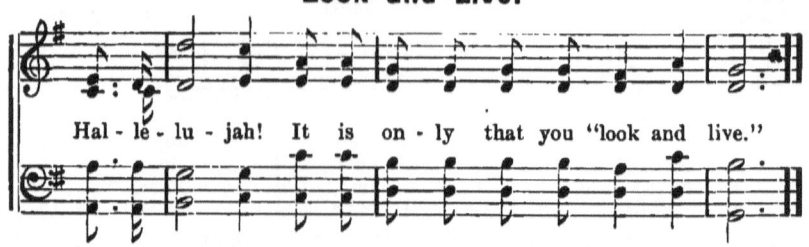

Hal-le-lu-jah! It is on-ly that you "look and live."

No. 9.   MY JESUS, I LOVE THEE.

A. J. Gordon,

1. My Je-sus, I love Thee, I know Thou art mine; For Thee all the
2. I love Thee, be-cause Thou Hast first lov-ed me, And purchased my
3. I'll love Thee in life, I will love Thee in death, And praise Thee as
4. In man-sions of glo-ry And end-less de-light, I'll ev-er a-

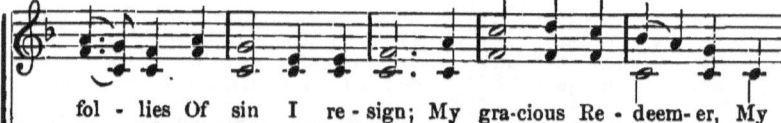

fol-lies Of sin I re-sign; My gra-cious Re-deem-er, My
par-don On Cal-va-ry's tree; I love Thee for wear-ing The
long as Thou lendest me breath; And say when the death-dew Lies
dore Thee In heav-en so bright; I'll sing with the glit-ter-ing

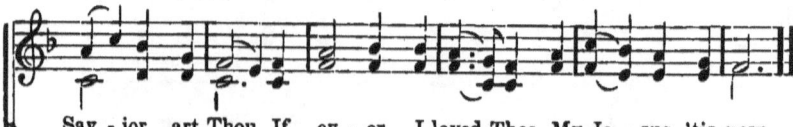

Sav-ior art Thou, If ev-er I loved Thee, My Je-sus, 'tis now.
thorns on Thy brow; If ev-er I loved Thee, My Je-sus, 'tis now.
cold on my brow, If ev-er I loved Thee, My Je-sus, 'tis now.
Crown on my brow, If ev-er I loved Thee, My Je-sus, 'tis now.

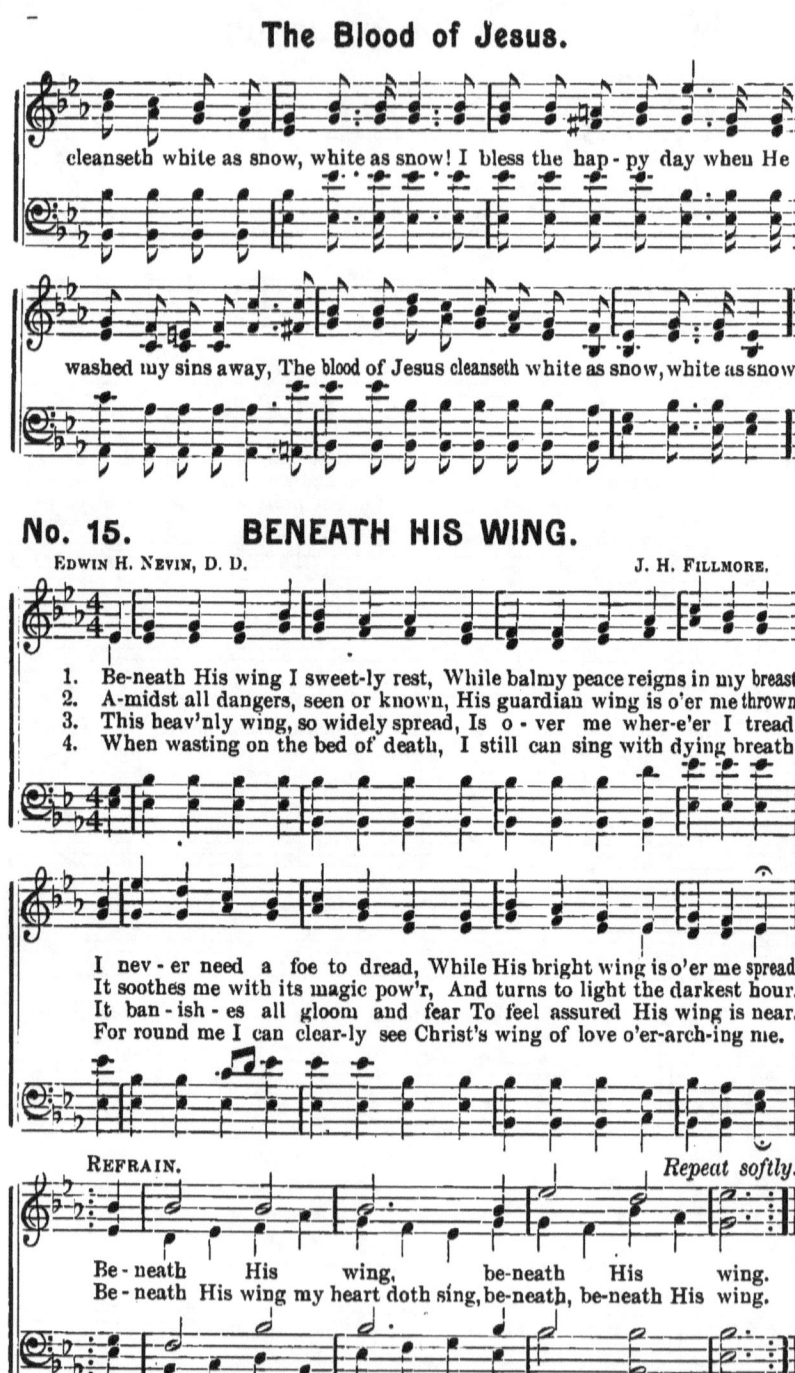

When the Roll is Called up Yonder.

yon - - der, When the roll .... is called up
yon-der, I'll be there, When the roll is called up

yon - der, When the roll is called up yon - der, I'll be there.

No. 21. HAVE MERCY.

1. A - las! and did my Sav - ior bleed, And did my Sovereign die?
2. Was it for crimes that I had done He groaned up - on the tree?
3. Well might the sun in dark - ness hide, And shut his glo - ries in,
4. Thus might I hide my blush - ing face While His dear cross ap - pears;
5. But drops of grief can ne'er re - pay The debt of love I owe;

Would He de - vote that sa - cred head For such a worm as I?
A - maz-ing pit - y, grace unknown, And love be-yond de - gree!
When Christ, the mighty Mak - er, died For man, the creature's sin.
Dis - solve my heart in thank - ful - ness, And melt mine eyes to tears.
Here, Lord, I give my - self a - way; 'Tis all that I can do.

CHORUS.

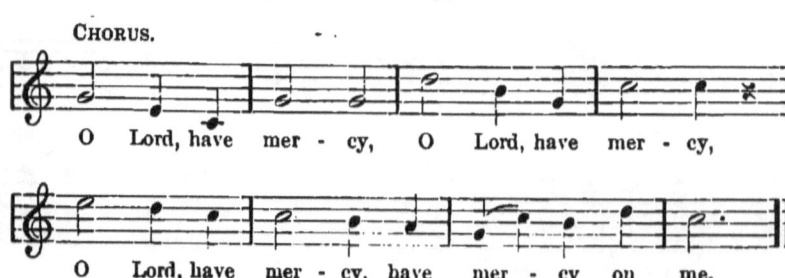

O Lord, have mer - cy, O Lord, have mer - cy,

O Lord, have mer - cy, have mer - cy on me.

No. 23. THIS NOTE SHALL SWELL.

(YORKSHIRE DOXOLOGY.)

Words and Melody furnished by Isaac Naylor.

1. I'll praise Thee, Savior, Prince of peace, In songs of praise that ne'er shall cease;
2. I'll praise Thee for the crimson flood, For cleansing in Thy precious blood;
3. I'll praise Thee for salvation's might, That turns my darkness in-to light;
4. I'll praise Thee when 'tis dark and drear, 'Mid sorrow's frowns I will not fear;
5. I'll praise Thee in a loft-y strain, I'll praise Thee in a sweet re-frain;
6. I'll praise Thee with my present breath, I'll praise Thee in the hour of death;

'Till time and life and tho't en-dure, I'll praise Thee, Sav-ior, ev-er-more.
I'll praise Thee for Thy Spirit's pow'r, That fills and keeps me hour by hour.
That scat-ters all my gloom and sin, I'll praise Thee, O, my Sav-ior King.
In dark-est night I'll raise my song, And roll the glo-rious strains a long.
I'll praise Thee more than tongue can tell, For Thou art do-ing all things well.
I'll praise Thee as I mount a-bove, I'll praise Thee in the realms of love.

CHORUS.

And above the rest this note shall swell, This note shall swell, this note shall swell,

And above the rest this note shall swell, My Jesus hath done all things well.

COPYRIGHT, 1893, BY CHAS. H. GABRIEL. ALL RIGHTS RESERVED.

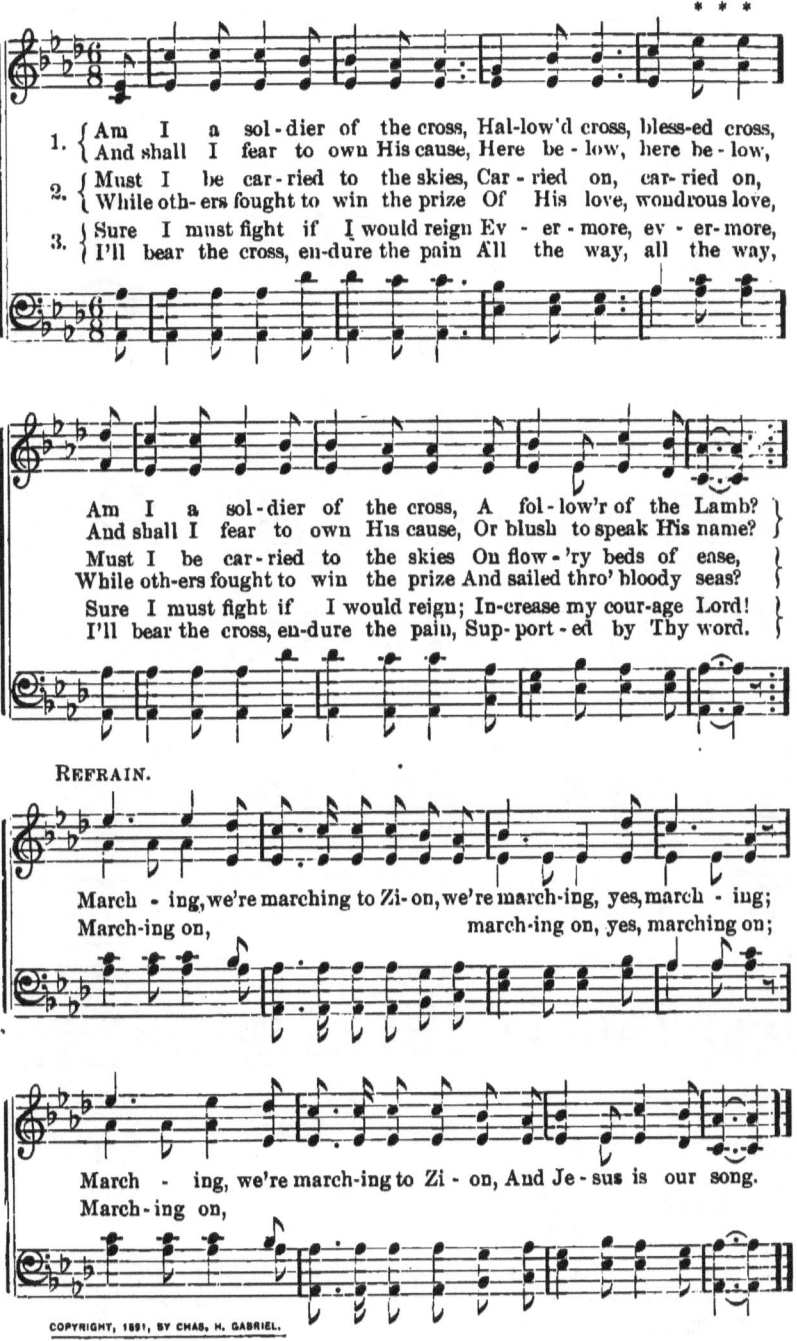

No. 28. BLIND BARTIMEUS.

Mrs. Joseph F. Knapp.

1. Whence Jesus came, I cannot tell, Nor why He came to me;
2. When all was dark, One touch'd my eyes, And that is all I know;
3. How it was done, I cannot say, Nor even think, nor dream;
4. It is the Son of God! His grace Makes trembling weakness strong;

One thing I know, and know it well, Tho' I was blind, I see!
For light came down from Paradise, And set my soul a-glow!
Nor why a touch of moistened clay Should make things what they seem.
Wipes tears away from sorrow's face, And teaches grief a song.

CHORUS. *Ad lib.*

I once was blind, but now I see! And that is news enough for me, And that is news enough for me.
I once was blind, but now I see! And that is light enough for me, And that is light enough for me.
I once was blind, but now I see! And that is truth enough for me, And that is truth enough for me.
I once was blind, but now I see! And that is joy enough for me, And that is joy enough for me.

A tempo.

COPYRIGHT, 1893, BY MRS. JOSEPH F. KNAPP.

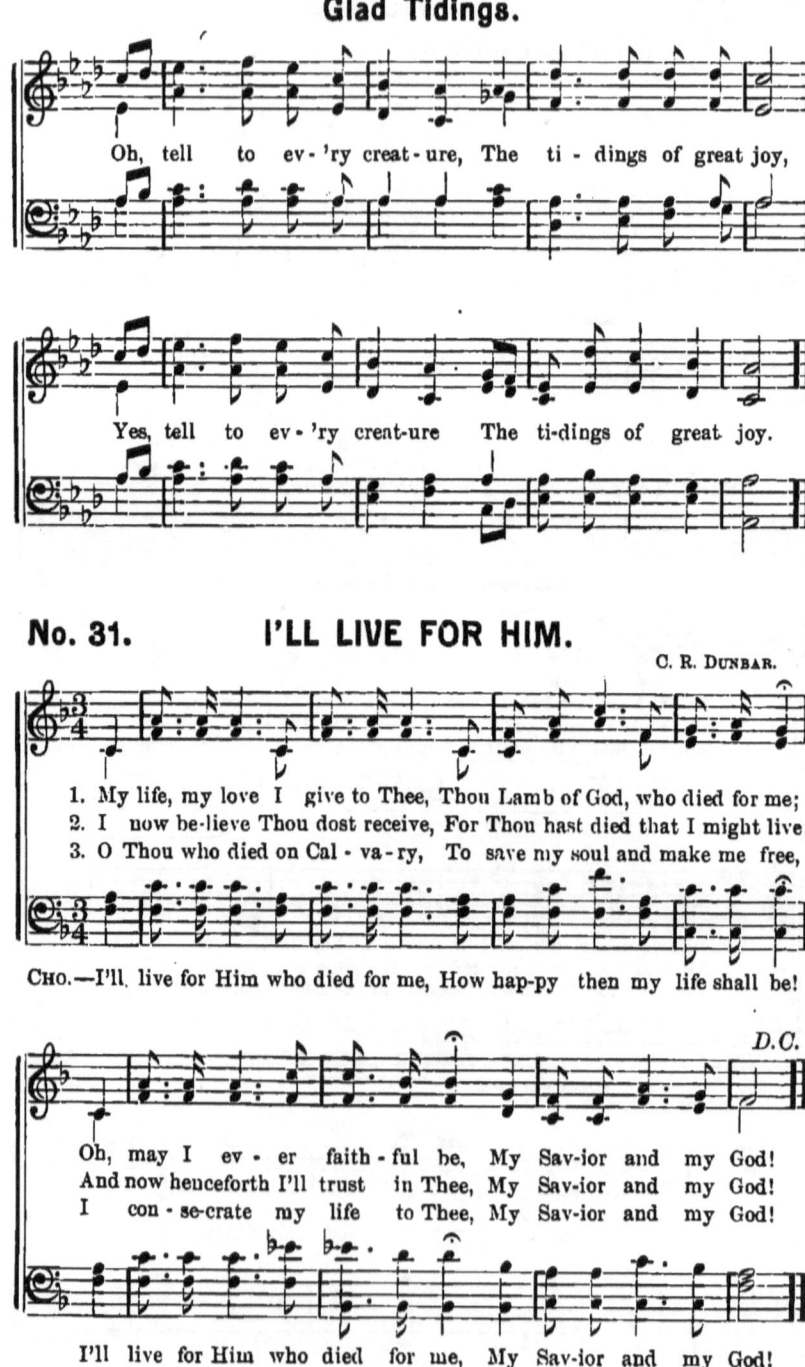

No. 32. HE REDEEMED ME.

F. G. Burroughs.   Geo. F. Rosche.

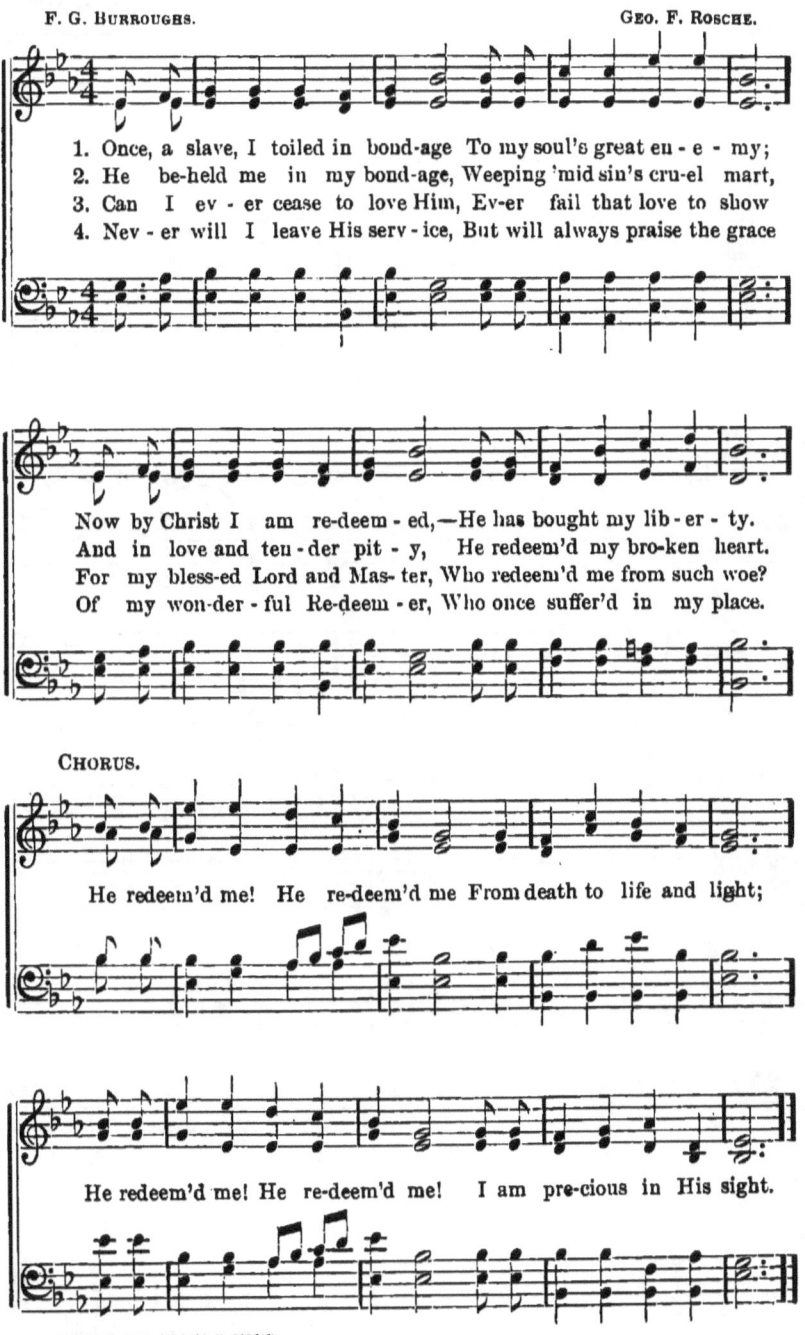

1. Once, a slave, I toiled in bond-age To my soul's great en-e-my;
2. He be-held me in my bond-age, Weeping 'mid sin's cru-el mart,
3. Can I ev-er cease to love Him, Ev-er fail that love to show
4. Nev-er will I leave His serv-ice, But will always praise the grace

Now by Christ I am re-deem-ed,—He has bought my lib-er-ty.
And in love and ten-der pit-y, He redeem'd my bro-ken heart.
For my bless-ed Lord and Mas-ter, Who redeem'd me from such woe?
Of my won-der-ful Re-deem-er, Who once suffer'd in my place.

CHORUS.

He redeem'd me! He re-deem'd me From death to life and light;

He redeem'd me! He re-deem'd me! I am pre-cious in His sight.

COPYRIGHT, 1894, BY CHAS. H. GABRIEL.

No. 34. BLESSED ASSURANCE.

FANNY J. CROSBY.   Mrs. J. F. KNAPP.

1. Bless-ed as-sur-ance, Je-sus is mine! Oh, what a fore-taste of glo-ry di-vine! Heir of sal-va-tion, purchased of God, Born of His Spir-it, wash'd in His blood.
2. Per-fect sub-mis-sion, Per-fect de-light, Vis-ions of rapt-ure burst now on my sight, An-gels de-scend-ing, bring from a-bove, Ech-oes of mer-cy, whis-pers of love.
3. Per-fect sub-mis-sion, All is at rest, I, in my Sav-ior, am hap-py and blest, Watch-ing and wait-ing, look-ing a-bove, Filled with His goodness, lost in His love.

CHORUS.

This is my sto-ry, this is my song, Praising my Sav-ior all the day long; This is my sto-ry, this is my song, Prais-ing my Sav-ior all the day long.

COPYRIGHT, 1873, BY JOS. F. KNAPP.

No. 36. UNDER THE BANNER OF LOVE.

Words and Melody furnished by Isaac Naylor.

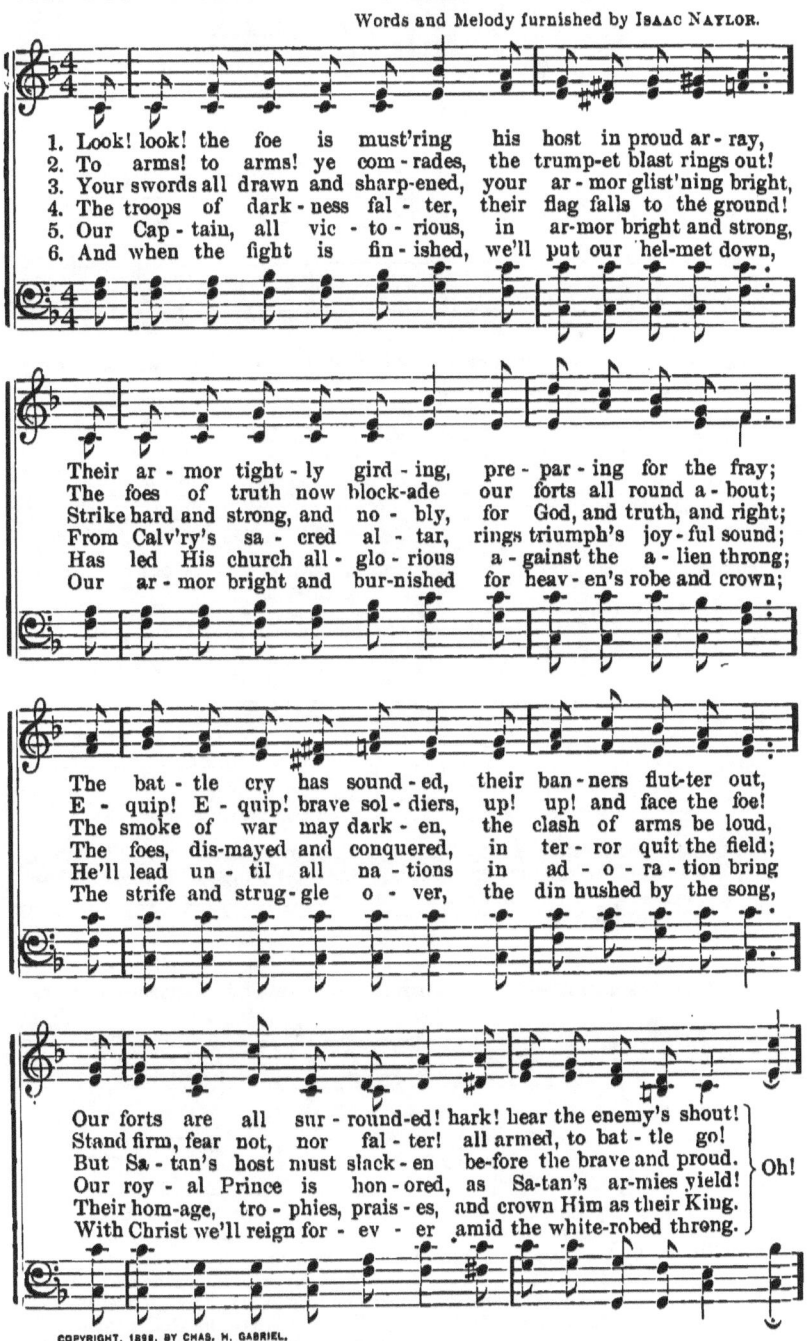

1. Look! look! the foe is must'ring his host in proud ar-ray, Their ar-mor tight-ly gird-ing, pre-par-ing for the fray; The bat-tle cry has sound-ed, their ban-ners flut-ter out, Our forts are all sur-round-ed! hark! hear the enemy's shout!
2. To arms! to arms! ye com-rades, the trump-et blast rings out! The foes of truth now block-ade our forts all round a-bout; E-quip! E-quip! brave sol-diers, up! up! and face the foe! Stand firm, fear not, nor fal-ter! all armed, to bat-tle go!
3. Your swords all drawn and sharp-ened, your ar-mor glist'ning bright, Strike hard and strong, and no-bly, for God, and truth, and right; The smoke of war may dark-en, the clash of arms be loud, But Sa-tan's host must slack-en be-fore the brave and proud.
4. The troops of dark-ness fal-ter, their flag falls to the ground! From Calv'ry's sa-cred al-tar, rings triumph's joy-ful sound; The foes, dis-mayed and conquered, in ter-ror quit the field; Our roy-al Prince is hon-ored, as Sa-tan's ar-mies yield!
5. Our Cap-tain, all vic-to-rious, in ar-mor bright and strong, Has led His church all-glo-rious a-gainst the a-lien throng; He'll lead un-til all na-tions in ad-o-ra-tion bring Their hom-age, tro-phies, prais-es, and crown Him as their King.
6. And when the fight is fin-ished, we'll put our hel-met down, Our ar-mor bright and bur-nished for heav-en's robe and crown; The strife and strug-gle o-ver, the din hushed by the song, With Christ we'll reign for-ev-er amid the white-robed throng.

Oh!

COPYRIGHT, 1898, BY CHAS. H. GABRIEL.

Under the Banner of Love.

CHORUS.

Un-der the banner of love we'll fight our way to glo-ry! Un-der the banner of love we'll conquer or we'll die! Un-der the banner of love we'll spread the gospel story; Our Je-sus and sal-va-tion shall be our battle cry.

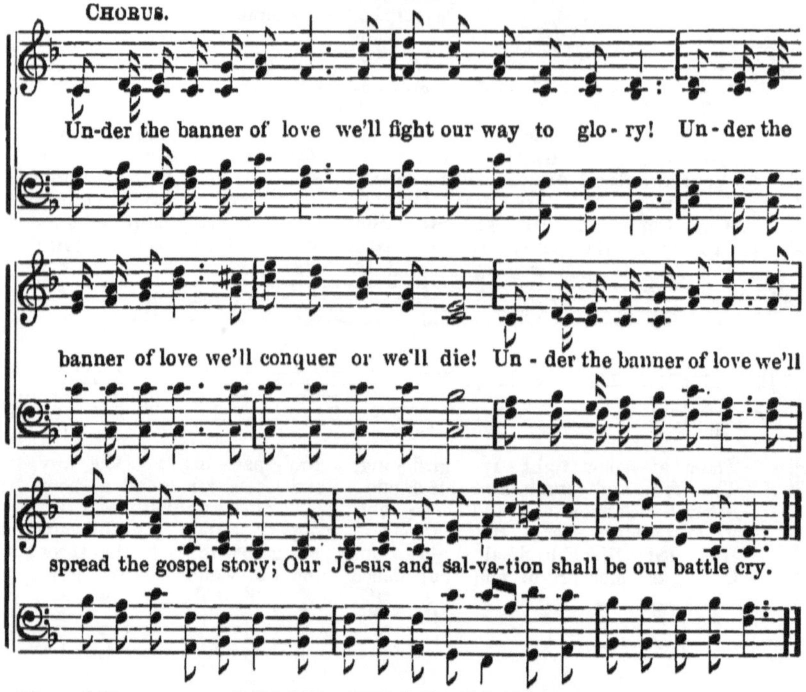

No. 37. COME, THOU FOUNT.

Rev. R. Robinson
John Wyeth FINE.

1. Come, Thou fount of ev-'ry bless-ing, Tune my heart to sing Thy grace;
   Streams of mer-cy, nev-er ceas-ing, Call for songs of loud-est praise;

D.C.—Praise the mount—I'm fixed upon it! Mount of Thy re-deem-ing love.

Teach me some mel-o-dious son-net, Sung by flam-ing tongues a-bove;

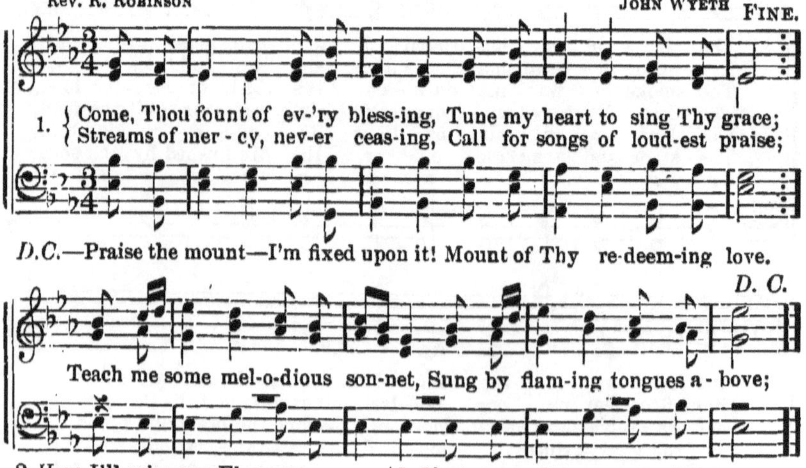

2 Here I'll raise my Ebenezer,
   Hither by Thy help I'm come;
  And I hope, by Thy good pleasure,
   Safely to arrive at home;
  Jesus sought me when a stranger,
   Wandering from the fold of God;
  He, to rescue me from danger,
   Interposed His precious blood.

3 Oh, to grace how great a debtor,
   Daily I'm constrained to be!
  Let Thy goodness, as a fetter,
   Bind my wandering heart to Thee;
  Prone to wander, Lord, I feel it—
   Prone to leave the God I love—
  Here's my heart, oh, take and seal it,
   Seal it for Thy courts above.

No. 40. LET NOT YOUR HEART BE TROUBLED.

Mrs. Ida M. Budd.   Chas. H. Gabriel.
Duet for Tenor and Alto.

1. "Let not your heart be troub-led," Oh, words of com-fort sweet! We
2. "Let not your heart be troub-led," Tho' dark the way may be; Cast
3. "Let not your heart be troub-led," For to His glorious home—The

bow, O bless-ed Sav-ior, A - dor-ing at Thy feet; Thy cheering words so
all thy care up-on Him, And He will care for thee. His wisdom still will
place He is pre-par-ing, His own at last shall come. Oh, teach us, lov-ing

ten - der, Our hearts would gladly heed; Our will-ing feet would
guide thee, His lov - ing hand up - hold; His mer - cy keep thee
Sav - ior, To walk the nar-row way; And all a - long the

CHORUS.

fol - low Where'er our Lord shall lead.)
ev - er, Safe, safe with-in His fold. } Let not your heart be troubled, Let
journey, Still may we hear Thee say:)

not your heart be troubled, As ye be-lieve in the Fa-ther, Be-

COPYRIGHT, 1894, BY CHAS. H. GABRIEL.

Let Not your Heart be Troubled.

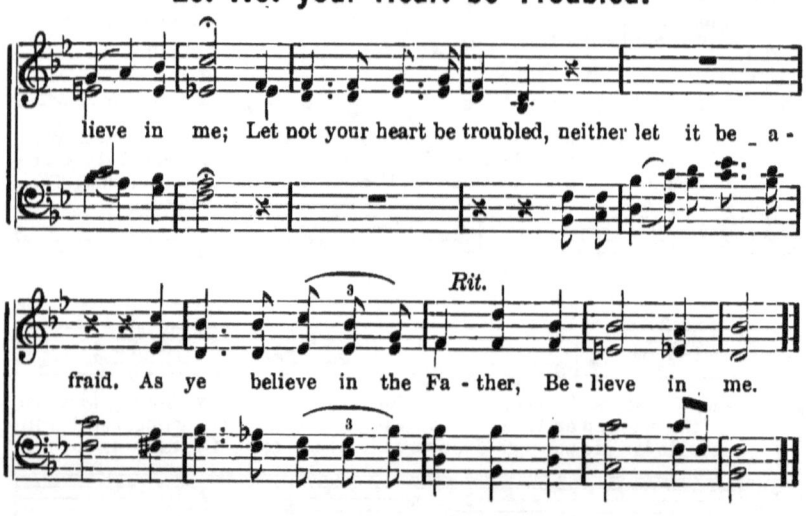

No. 41. JUST AS I AM.

Charlotte Elliott. Wm. B. Bradbury.

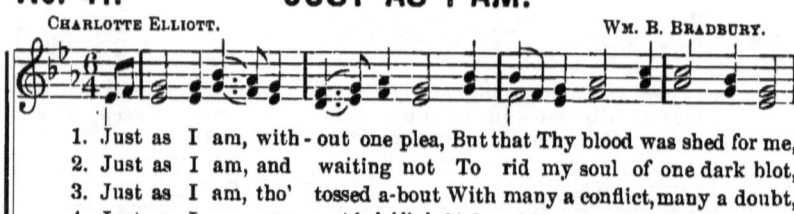

1. Just as I am, with-out one plea, But that Thy blood was shed for me,
2. Just as I am, and waiting not To rid my soul of one dark blot,
3. Just as I am, tho' tossed a-bout With many a conflict, many a doubt,
4. Just as I am—poor, wretched, blind, Sight, rich-es, healing of the mind,
5. Just as I am—Thou wilt receive, Wilt welcome, pardon, cleanse, relieve;
6. Just as I am—Thy love unknown Hath broken ev-'ry bar-rier down;

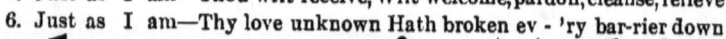

And that Thou bidd'st me come to Thee, O Lamb of God, I come! I come!
To Thee whose blood can cleanse each spot, O Lamb of God, I come! I come!
Fightings with-in, and fears without, O Lamb of God, I come! I come!
Yea, all I need, in Thee to find, O Lamb of God, I come! I come!
Be - cause Thy prom-ise I be-lieve, O Lamb of God, I come! I come!
Now, to be Thine, yea, Thine a-lone, O Lamb of God, I come! I come!

No. 44. I AM TRUSTING THEE.

F. R. Havergal.
Dr. S. B. Jackson.

1. I am trust-ing Thee, Lord Je-sus, Trust-ing on - ly Thee;
2. I am trust-ing Thee for par - don, At Thy feet I bow,
3. I am trust-ing Thee for cleans-ing In the crim - son flood;
4. I am trust-ing Thee to guide me; Thou a - lone shalt lead,
5. I am trust-ing Thee, Lord Je - sus, Nev - er let me fall.

Trust-ing Thee for full sal - va - tion, Great and free.
For Thy grace and ten - der par - don Trust - ing now.
Trust-ing Thee to make me ho - ly By Thy blood.
Ev - 'ry day and hour sup - ply - ing All my need.
I am trust - ing Thee for - ev - er, And for all.

REFRAIN.

I am trust-ing Thee, Lord Je-sus, I am trust-ing on - ly Thee,

I am trusting Thee, fully trusting Thee; I am trust-ing on - ly Thee.

COPYRIGHT, 1894, BY CHAS. H. GABRIEL.

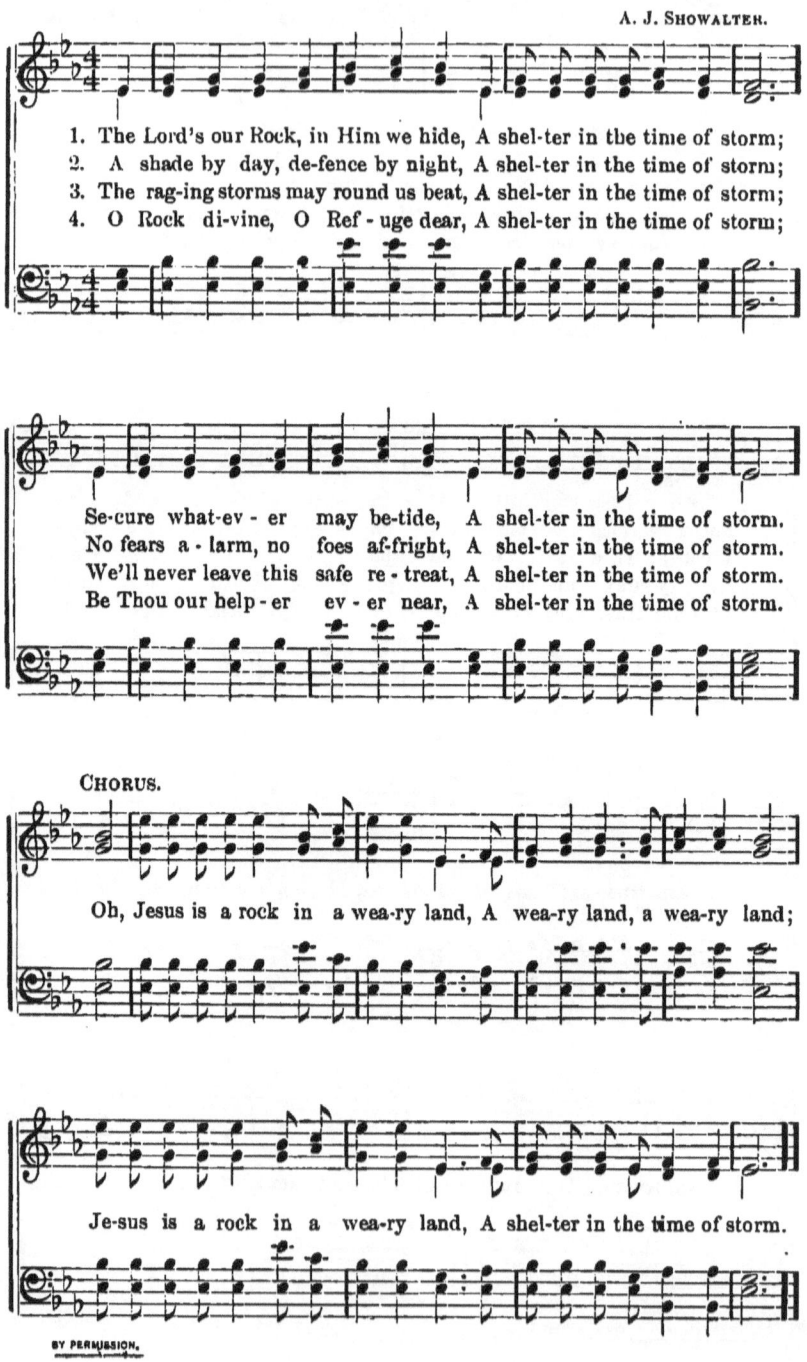

No. 46. LEAD ME, SAVIOR.

F. M. D. | FRANK M. DAVIS.

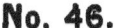

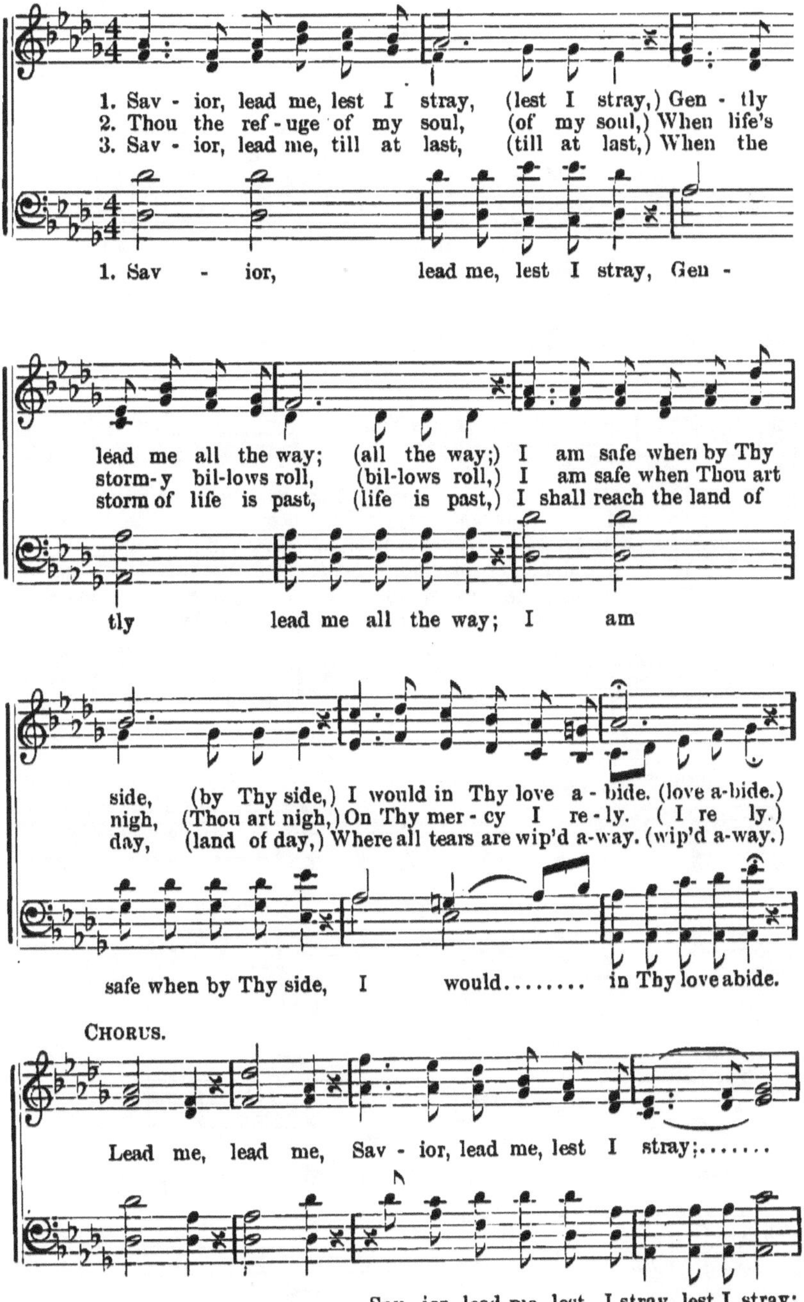

BY PERMISSION

Lead Me, Savior.

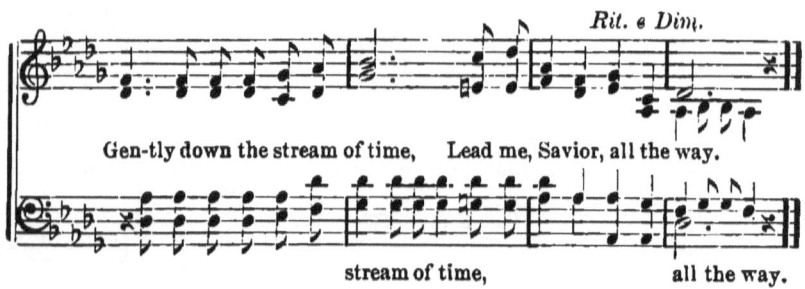

Gen-tly down the stream of time, Lead me, Savior, all the way.
stream of time, all the way.

No. 47. THY WILL BE DONE.

W. H. GARDNER.   EDWIN MOORE.

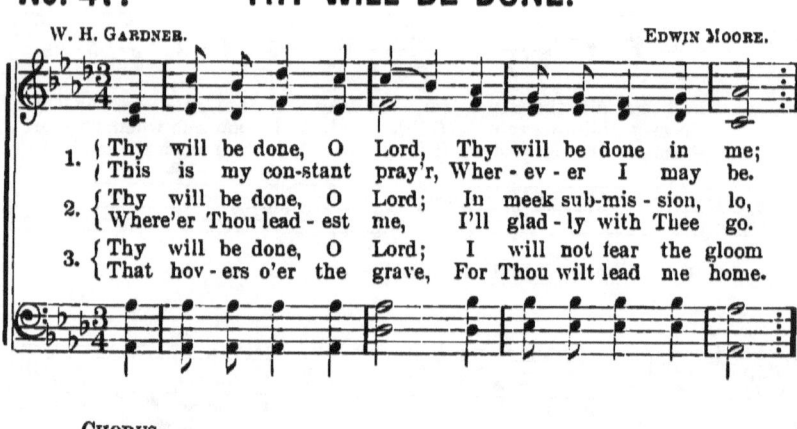

1. Thy will be done, O Lord, Thy will be done in me;
   This is my con-stant pray'r, Wher-ev-er I may be.
2. Thy will be done, O Lord; In meek sub-mis-sion, lo,
   Where'er Thou lead-est me, I'll glad-ly with Thee go.
3. Thy will be done, O Lord; I will not fear the gloom
   That hov-ers o'er the grave, For Thou wilt lead me home.

CHORUS.

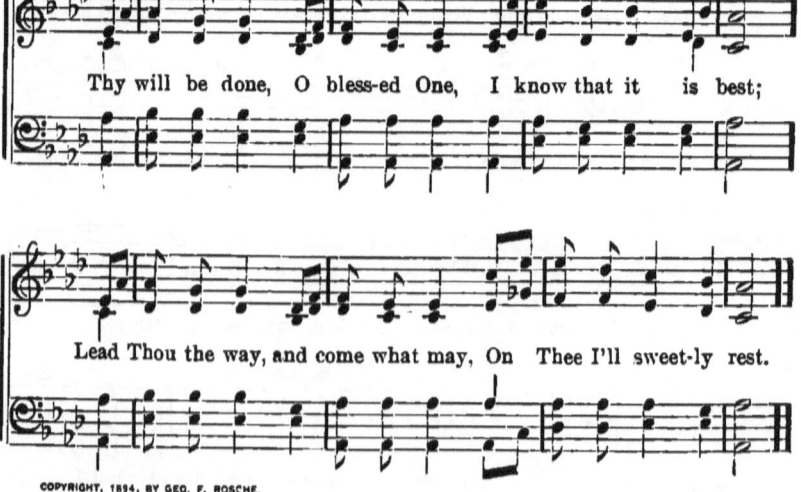

Thy will be done, O bless-ed One, I know that it is best;
Lead Thou the way, and come what may, On Thee I'll sweet-ly rest.

COPYRIGHT, 1894, BY GEO. F. ROSCHE.

No. 48. "I LONG TO BEHOLD HIM."

C. WESLEY.　　　　　　　　　　　　　　　　　　　T. C. O'KANE.

1. I long to behold Him arrayed With glo-ry and light from above,
2. I languish and sigh to be there, Where Jesus hath fixed His a-bode;
3. With Him I on Zi-on shall stand, For Je-sus hath spoken the word,
4. But when, on Thy bosom reclined, Thy face I am strengthened to see,

The King in His beau-ty displayed, His beau-ty of ho-li-est love.
Oh, when shall we meet in the air, And fly to the mountain of God!
The breadth of Im-man-uel's land Sur-vey by the light of my Lord.
My full-ness of rap-ture I find, My heav-en of heavens in Thee.

CHORUS.

When the storms　　　all are o'er,　　　I shall see Him on that
When the storms, when the storms all are o'er, all are o'er, I shall see Him on that

beau-ti-ful shore,........ When the storms　　　all are
beau-ti-ful shore by and by, When the storms all are o'er　in the

o'er,.　　I shall see Him on that beau-ti-ful shore.
sweet by and by, I shall see Him on that beau-ti-ful shore by and by.

BY PERMISSION.

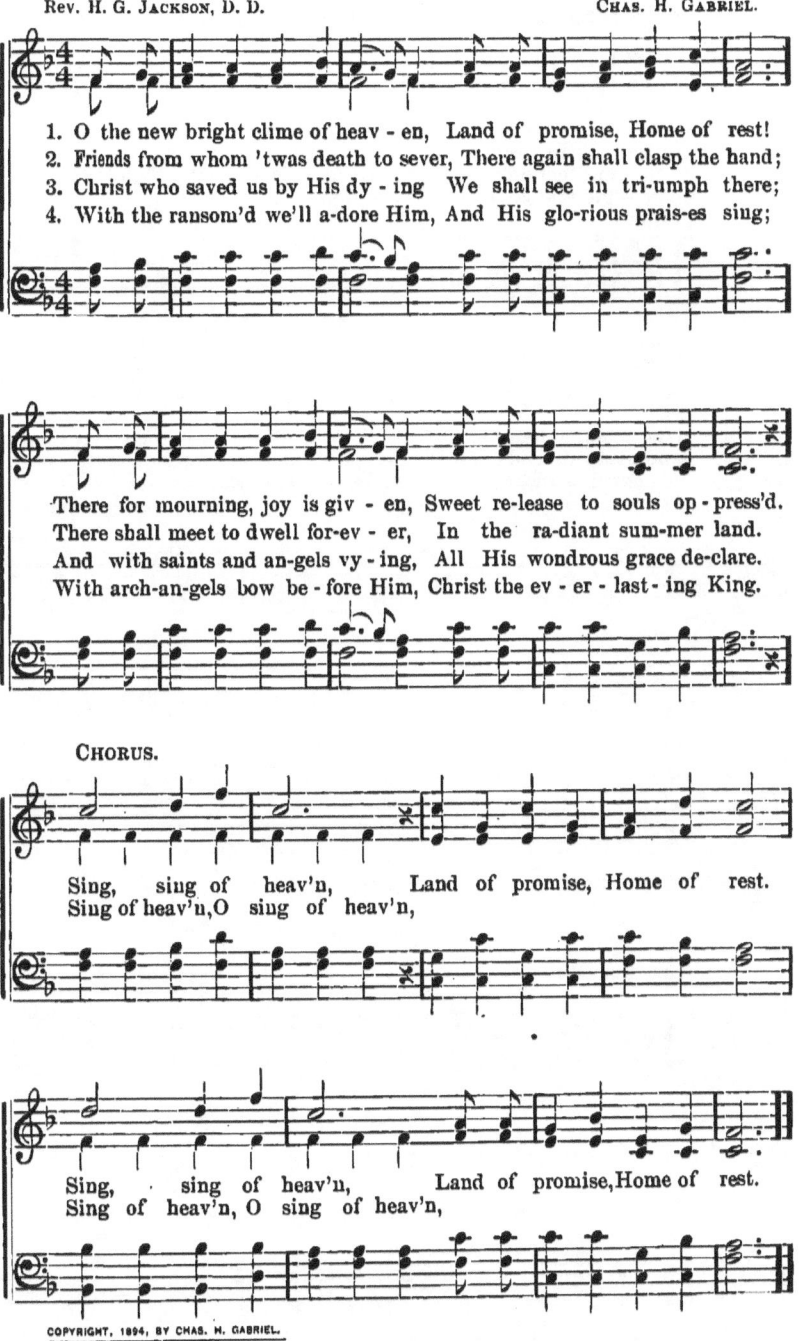

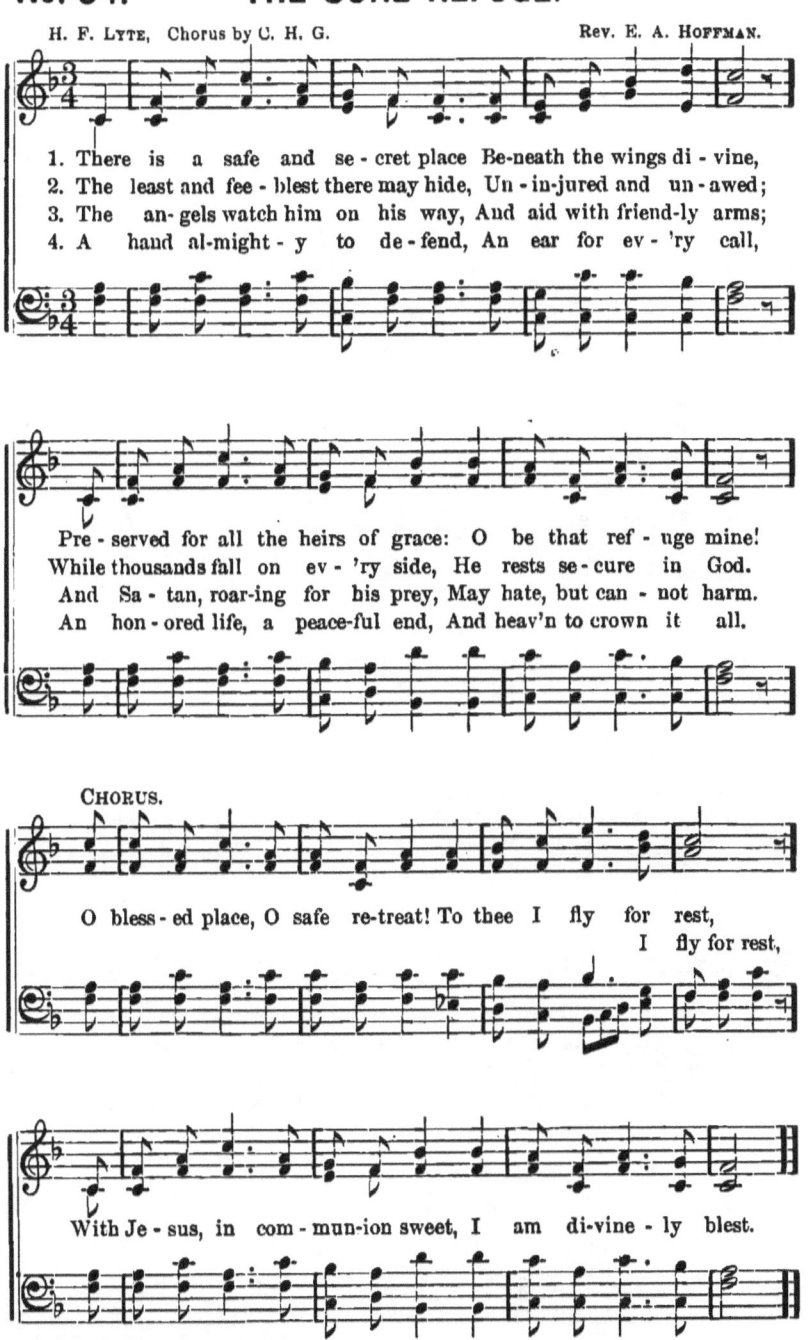

No. 55. SINGING FOR JESUS.

Rev. WM. APPEL.   CHAS. H. GABRIEL.

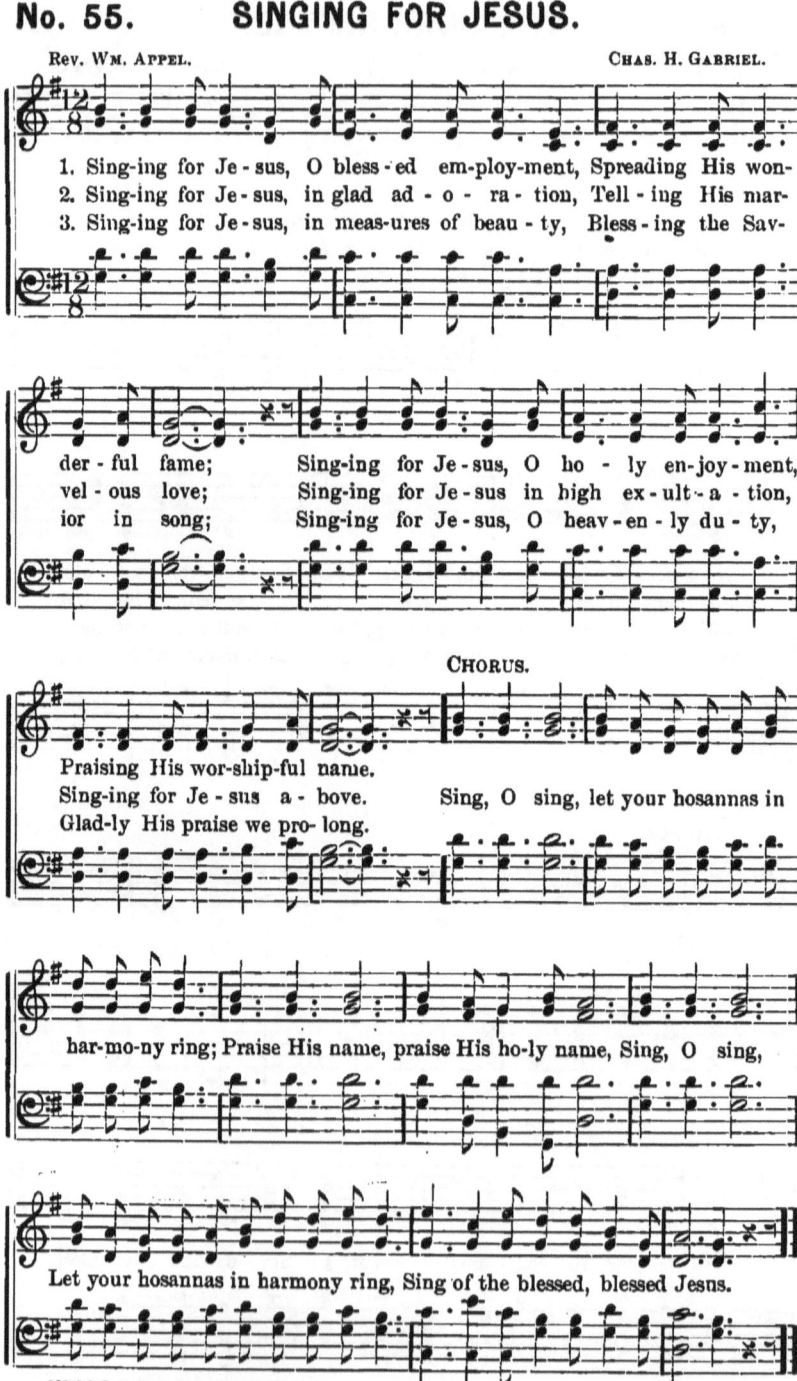

1. Sing-ing for Je-sus, O bless-ed em-ploy-ment, Spreading His won-der-ful fame;
2. Sing-ing for Je-sus, in glad ad-o-ra-tion, Tell-ing His mar-vel-ous love;
3. Sing-ing for Je-sus, in meas-ures of beau-ty, Bless-ing the Sav-ior in song;

Sing-ing for Je-sus, O ho-ly en-joy-ment, Praising His wor-ship-ful name.
Sing-ing for Je-sus in high ex-ult-a-tion, Sing-ing for Je-sus a-bove.
Sing-ing for Je-sus, O heav-en-ly du-ty, Glad-ly His praise we pro-long.

CHORUS.

Sing, O sing, let your hosannas in har-mo-ny ring; Praise His name, praise His ho-ly name, Sing, O sing, Let your hosannas in harmony ring, Sing of the blessed, blessed Jesus.

COPYRIGHT, 1892, BY CHAS. H. GABRIEL.

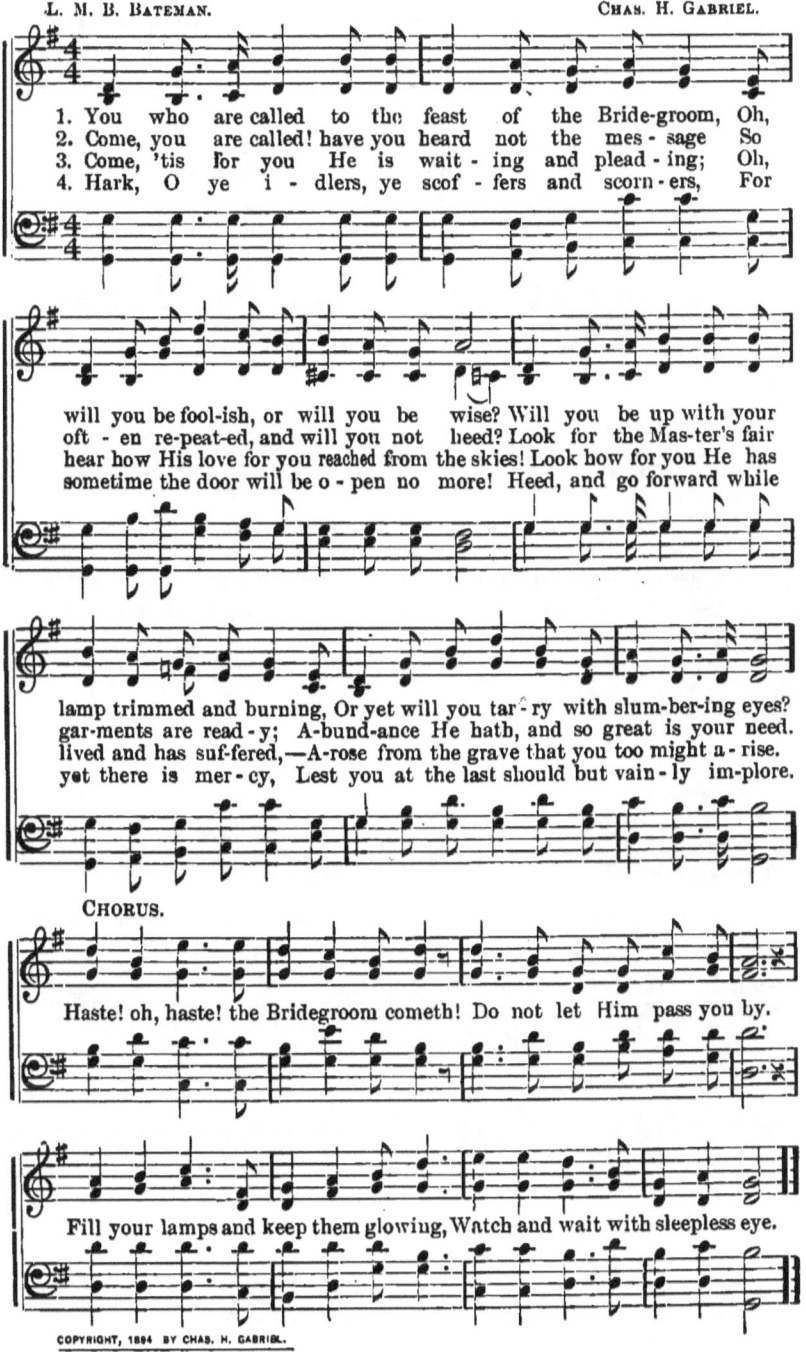

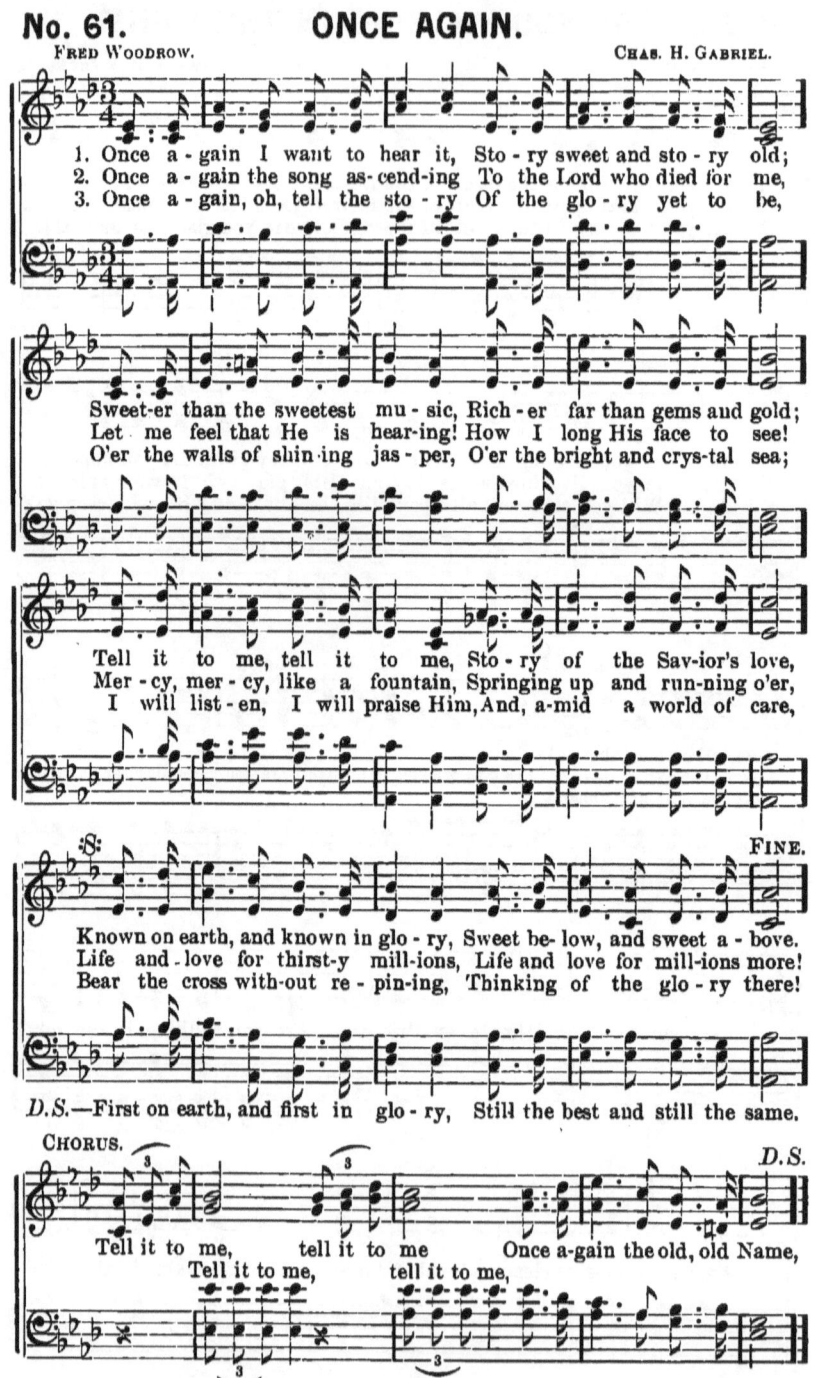

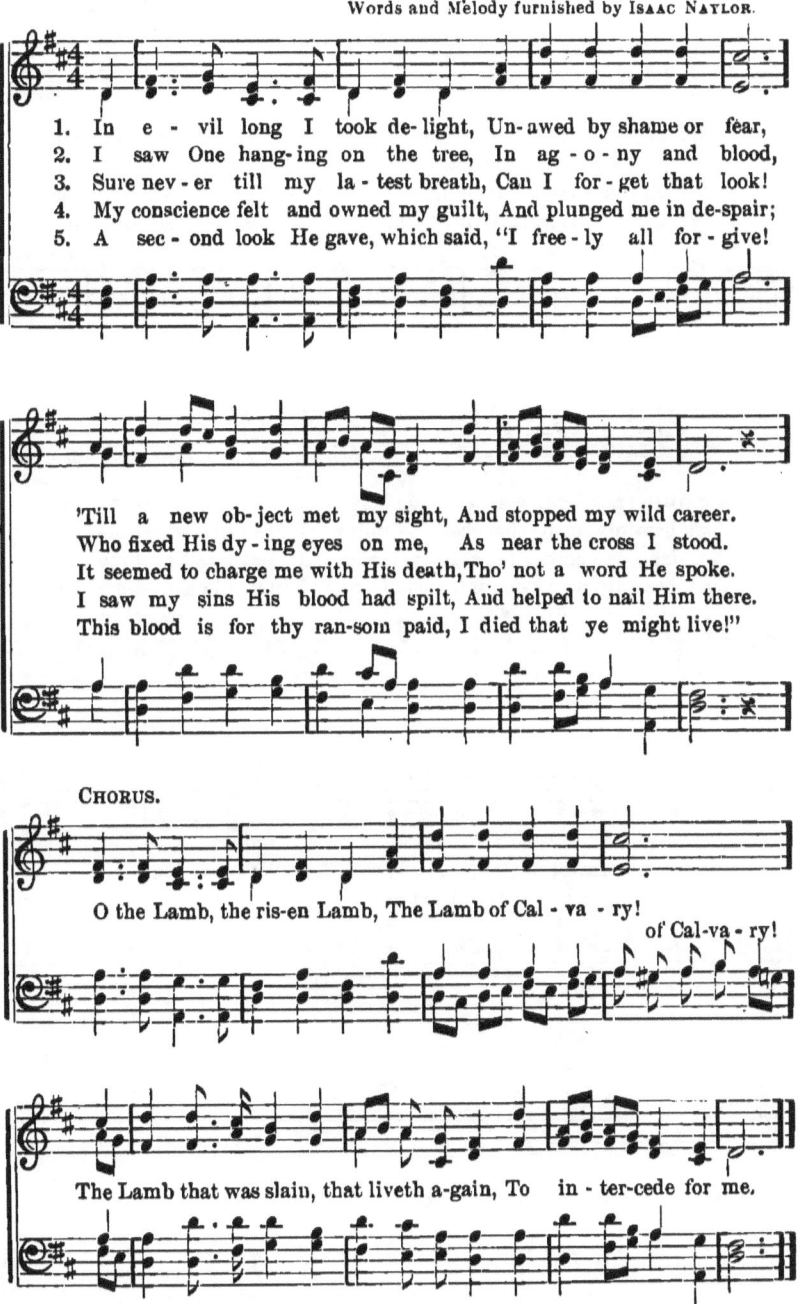

No. 64. ONLY FOR THEE.

F. G. Burroughs. Chas. H. Gabriel.

1. Bless-ed Redeem-er, great is Thy love, To give Thy life as a ransom for me! Now for Thy serv-ice I henceforth will live,
2. No earth-ly pleas-ure tempteth my soul, All I de-sire, lo, is hid-den in Thee! Naught but Thy presence can fill me with joy,
3. Frail is the ves-sel, yet for Thy use, Filled with Thy spir-it, I dai-ly may be; Per-fect in weak-ness Thy strength shall be made,
4. Small is the off'ring, fee-ble my praise, Yet, blessed Lord, all I have is for Thee; 'Tis but Thine own, e'en the all that I give;

Chorus.

On-ly for Thee I'll live, on-ly for Thee! On-ly for Thee I live, On-ly for Thee; Thou who didst die to save e-ven me; All that I have to Thy serv-ice I give, On-ly for Thee I live, on-ly for Thee!

Copyright, 1894, by Chas. H. Gabriel.

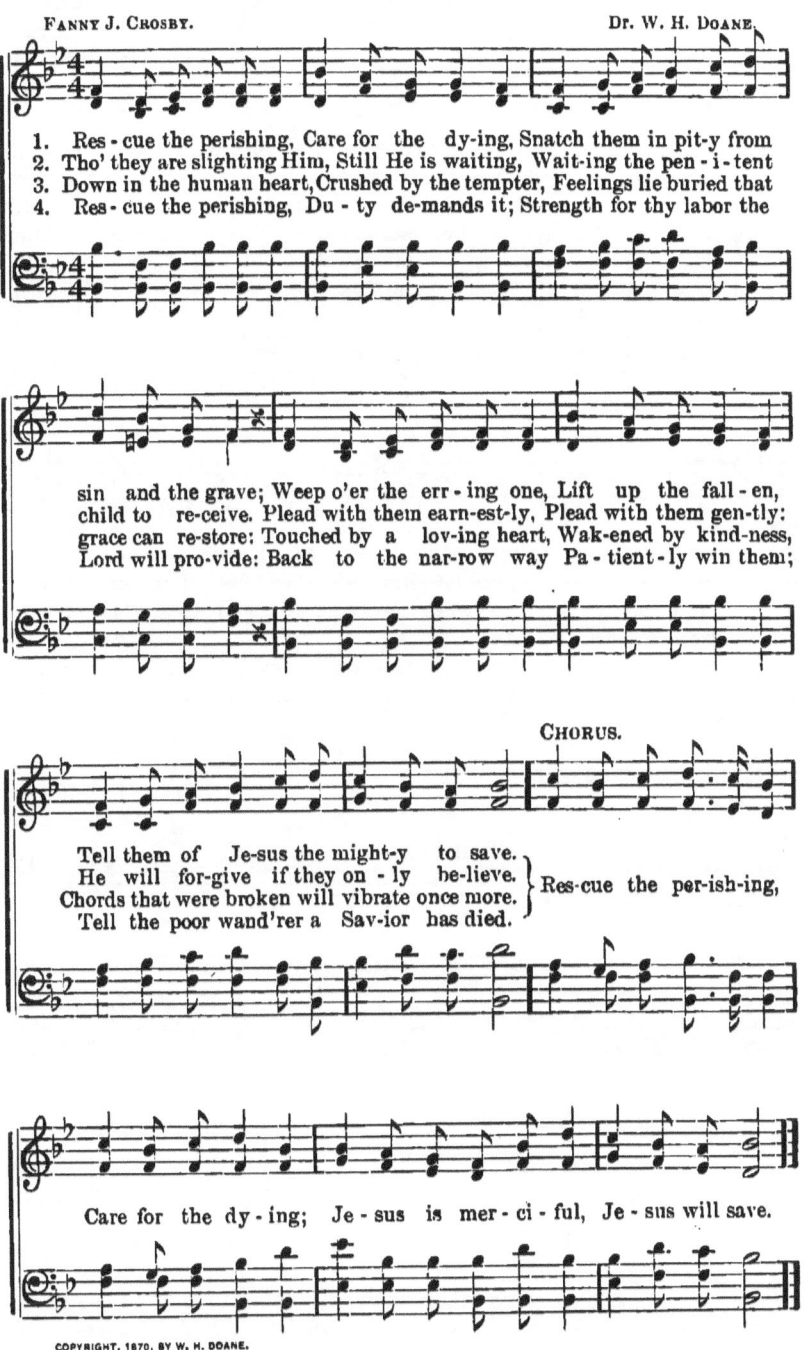

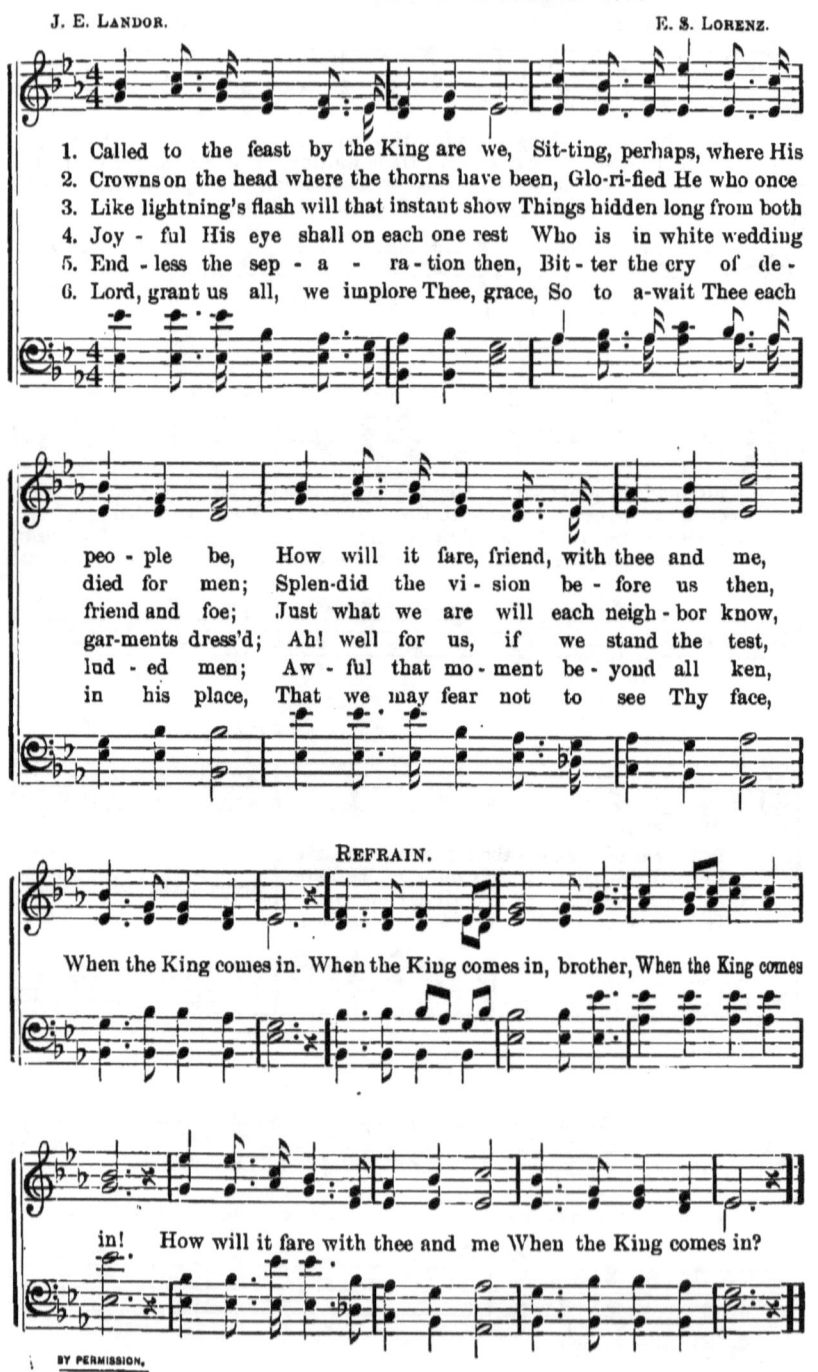

No. 73. SINNERS ARE COMING HOME.

C. H. G.   Chas. H. Gabriel.

1. Let mountains and hills with joy re-sound, And ech - o the spa-cious
2. Was ev - er a song so full and sweet, Was ev - er a sto - ry
3. Let heav - en with hal - le - lu - jahs ring, And an - gels in joy - ous
4. All glo - ry and praise to Je - sus give, For all may a - bund-ant

world a-round; The dead is a - live, the lost is found, And
so com-plete As that of the blood-bought mer - cy seat When
rap - ture sing The tri-umphs of Je - sus Christ the King, While
grace re - ceive; A soul from the depths may look and live, For

CHORUS.

sin-ners are com - ing home. Sin-ners are com-ing home,......
                                                   com - ing home,

Sin - ners are com - ing home!...... Glo - ry we sing to
                     com - ing home!

Je - sus our King, For sin - ners are com - ing home......
                                                           com - ing home.

He Leads and Guides Me.

Sweet peace and rest, Sweet peace and rest.
I find in Him sweet peace and rest,

No. 75. CLINGING TO THE CROSS.

ISAAC NAYLOR. For this work.

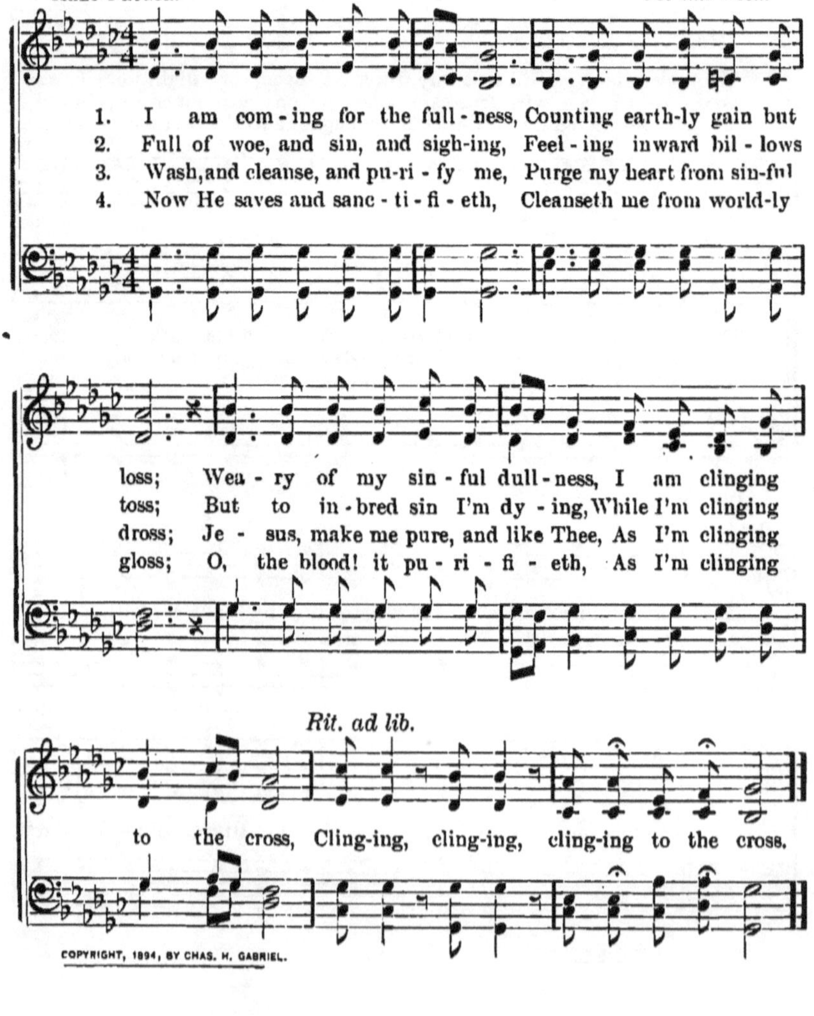

1. I am com-ing for the full-ness, Counting earth-ly gain but loss; Wea-ry of my sin-ful dull-ness, I am clinging
2. Full of woe, and sin, and sigh-ing, Feel-ing inward bil-lows toss; But to in-bred sin I'm dy-ing, While I'm clinging
3. Wash, and cleanse, and pu-ri-fy me, Purge my heart from sin-ful dross; Je-sus, make me pure, and like Thee, As I'm clinging
4. Now He saves and sanc-ti-fi-eth, Cleanseth me from world-ly gloss; O, the blood! it pu-ri-fi-eth, As I'm clinging

Rit. ad lib.

to the cross, Cling-ing, cling-ing, cling-ing to the cross.

COPYRIGHT, 1894, BY CHAS. H. GABRIEL.

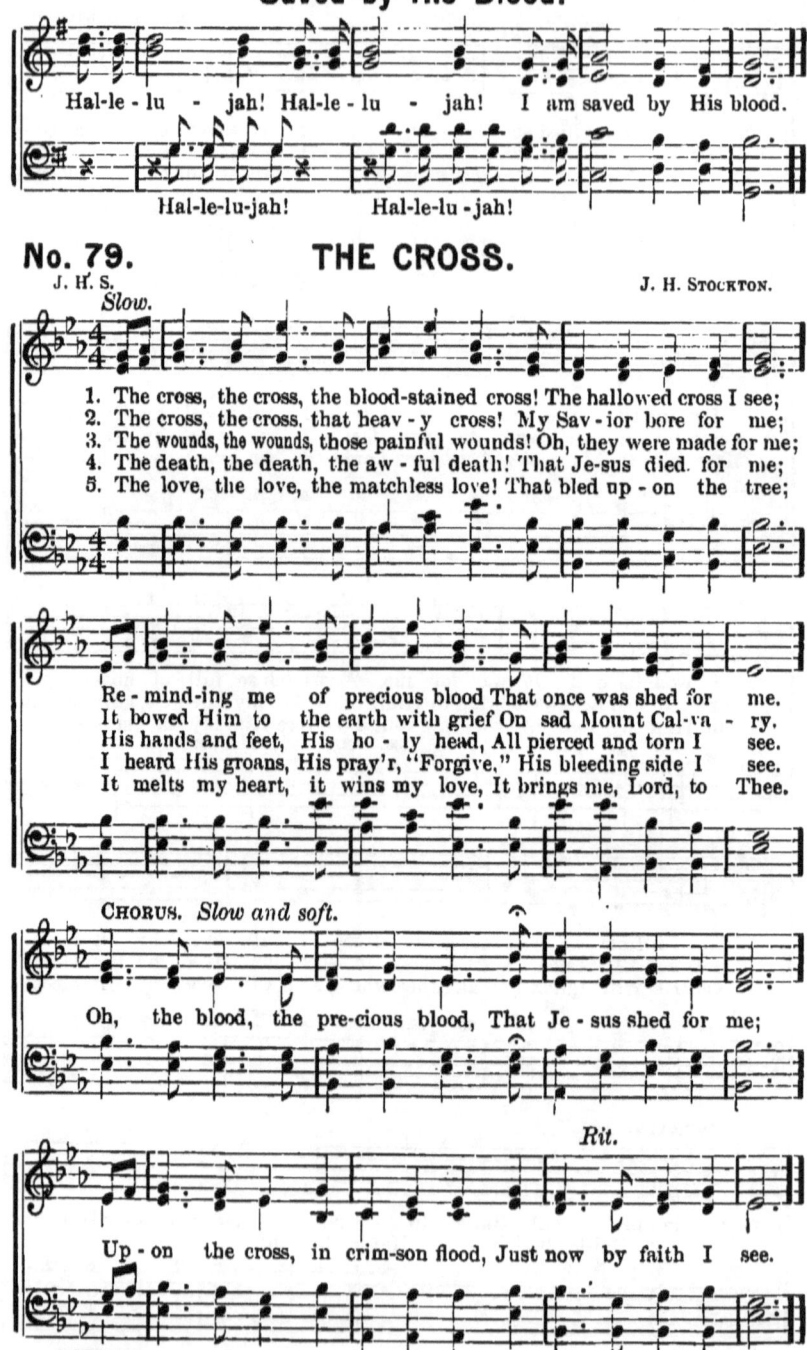

Praise the Lord.

No. 85. WORK FOR THE NIGHT.
Key of F.

1 Work, for the night is coming;
　Work through the morning hours;
　Work, while the dew is sparkling;
　Work, 'mid springing flowers;
　Work, when the day grows brighter,
　Work, in the glowing sun;
　Work, for the night is coming,
　When man's work is done.

2 Work, for the night is coming;
　Work through the sunny noon;
　Fill brightest hours with labor;
　Rest comes sure and soon.
　Give every flying minute
　Something to keep in store;
　Work, for the night is coming,
　When man works no more.

3 Work, for the night is coming,
　Under the sunset skies;
　While their bright tints are glowing,
　Work, for daylight flies.
　Work, till the last beam fadeth,
　Fadeth to shine no more;
　Work, while the night is dark'ning,
　When man's work is o'er.

No. 86. STAND UP FOR JESUS.
Tune:—WEBB.

1 Stand up! stand up for Jesus!
　Ye soldiers of the cross;
　Lift high His royal banner,
　It must not suffer loss;
　From victory unto victory
　His army He shall lead,
　Till every foe is vanquished,
　And Christ is Lord indeed.

2 Stand up! stand up for Jesus!
　Stand in His strength alone;
　The arm of flesh will fail you—
　Ye dare not trust your own;
　Put on the gospel armor,
　And, watching unto prayer,
　Where duty calls, or danger,
　Be never wanting there.

3 Stand up! stand up for Jesus!
　The strife will not be long;
　This day the noise of battle,
　The next the victor's song;
　To him that overcometh,
　A crown of life shall be;
　He with the King of glory
　Shall reign eternally.

No. 87. SAVED BY FAITH.

I. B.
Rev. Is. Baltzell.

1. I have found redemption in the Savior's blood, I am saved by faith in His
2. Oh, how sweet the story of His wondrous grace, I am saved by faith in His
3. I will sing of Je-sus while the days go by, I am saved by faith in His
4. I will keep on sing-ing as I march a-long, I am saved by faith in His

blood, in His blood; I am sweetly trust-ing in the word of God, I am
blood, in His blood; I will trust in Je-sus while I run my race, I am
blood, in His blood; I will trust His promise, on His strength re-ly, I am
blood, in His blood; In my home in glo-ry this shall be my song, I am

CHORUS.

saved by faith in His blood. I am saved,...... yes, sweetly saved,
I am saved, sweetly saved, I am saved, sweetly saved,

I am saved by faith in the blood He shed for me, I am saved by faith in His blood, in His blood.

BY PERMISSION.

Near to Thee.

Hold my hand in Thine, dear Sav-ior, Lead, oh, lead me all the way.

No. 92. JESUS, I MY CROSS HAVE TAKEN.

HENRY F. LYTE.   MOZART.

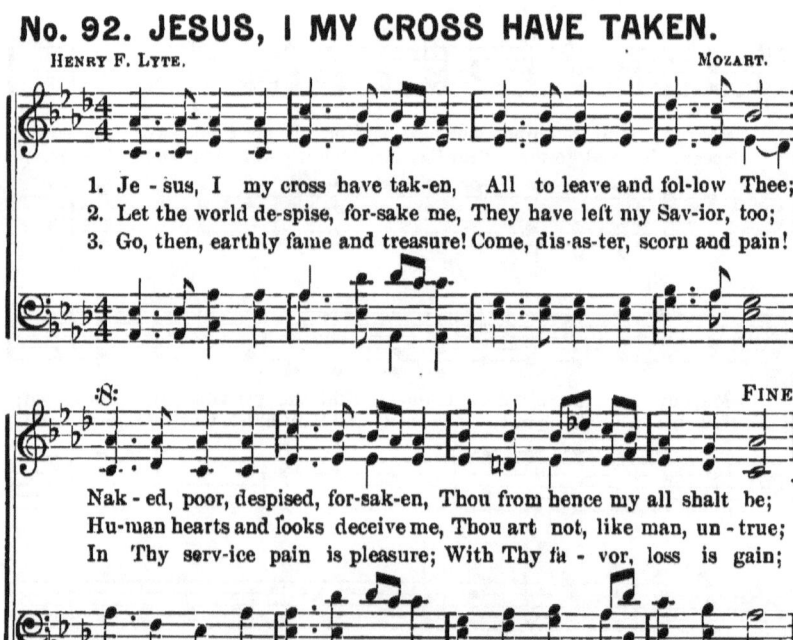

1. Je-sus, I my cross have tak-en, All to leave and fol-low Thee;
2. Let the world de-spise, for-sake me, They have left my Sav-ior, too;
3. Go, then, earthly fame and treasure! Come, dis-as-ter, scorn and pain!

Nak-ed, poor, despised, for-sak-en, Thou from hence my all shalt be;
Hu-man hearts and looks deceive me, Thou art not, like man, un-true;
In Thy serv-ice pain is pleasure; With Thy fa-vor, loss is gain;

D.S.—Yet how rich is my con-di-tion, God and heav'n are still my own.
Foes may hate, and friends may shun me, Show Thy face and all is bright.
Storms may howl and clouds may gather, All must work for good to me.

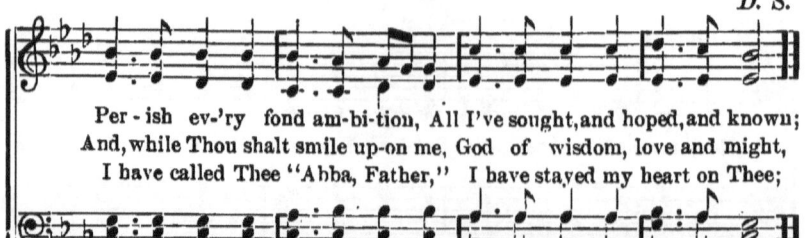

Per-ish ev-'ry fond am-bi-tion, All I've sought, and hoped, and known;
And, while Thou shalt smile up-on me, God of wisdom, love and might,
I have called Thee "Abba, Father," I have stayed my heart on Thee;

No. 93. SOURCE OF EVERY BLESSING.

Ralph Wardlow.   H. A. Henry.

1. Christ, of all my hopes the ground, Christ, the spring of all my joy;
2. Firm-ly trust-ing in Thy blood, Nothing shall my heart confound;

Still in Thee may I be found, Still for Thee my pow'rs employ.
Safe-ly I shall pass the flood, Safe-ly reach Im-man-uel's ground.

Fountain of o'er-flow-ing grace, Free-ly from Thy full-ness give;
When I touch the bless-ed shore, Back the clos-ing waves shall roll,

Till I close my earth-ly race, May I prove it "Christ to live!"
Death's dark stream shall nev-er-more Part from Thee my rav-ished soul.

CHORUS.

Thou art the source of ev-'ry bless-ing,
Thou art the source.......... of ev-'ry bless - - - ing,

COPYRIGHT, 1894, BY CHAS H GABRIEL.

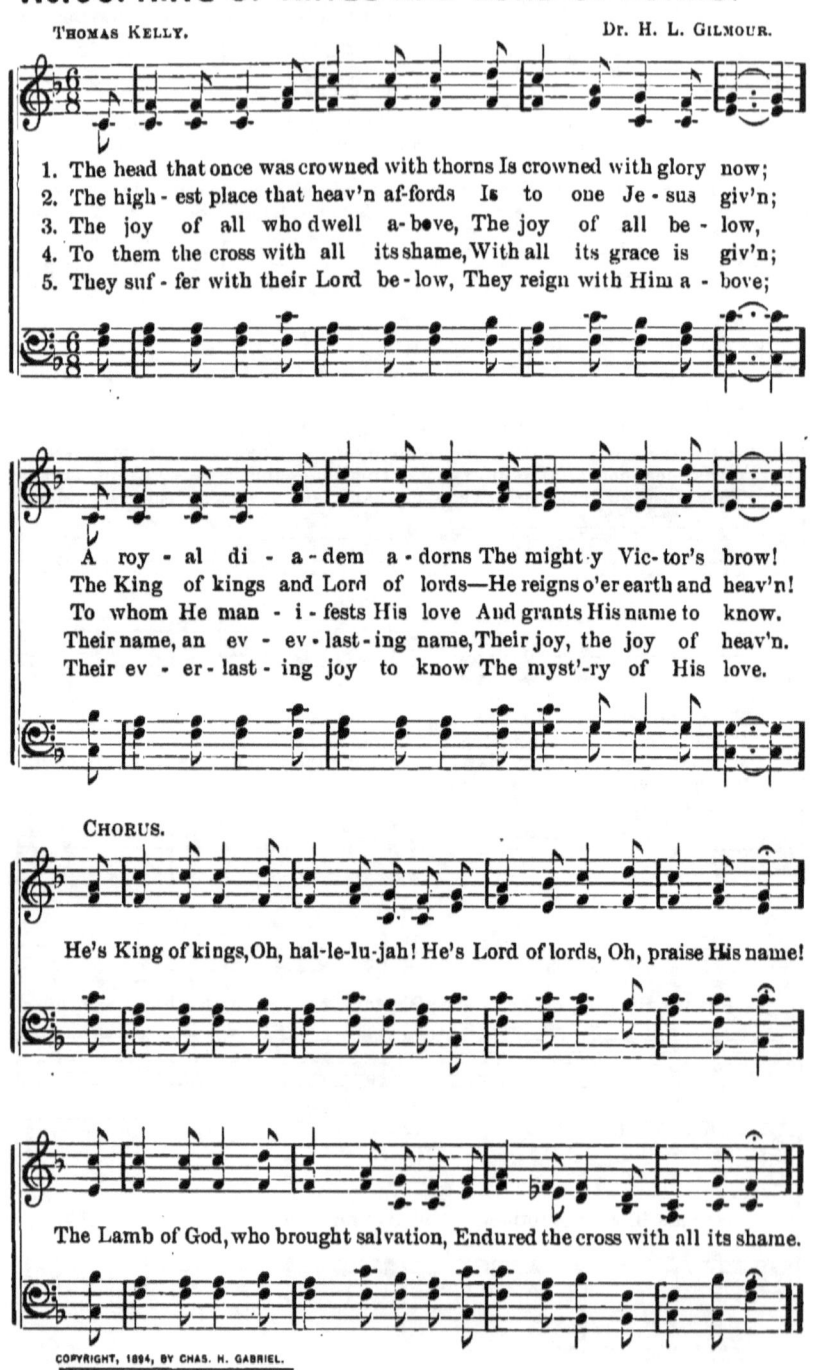

He Leaves It All With Thee.

For the fountain flow-eth free,...... 'Tis a won - - drous in - vi -
flow-eth free, 'Tis a won - drous, a
ta - tion, And He leaves it all with thee............
wondrous in - vi-ta - tion, He leaves it all with thee.

No. 98. ZION.

1. Guide me, O Thou great Jehovah!
   Pilgrim through this barren land,
   I am weak, but Thou art mighty;
   Hold me with Thy powerful hand:
   Bread of heaven,
   Feed me till I want no more.

2. Open now the crystal fountain,
   Whence the healing waters flow;
   Let the fiery, cloudy pillar
   Lead me all my journey through:
   Strong Deliverer,
   Be Thou still my strength and shield

3. When I tread the verge of Jordan,
   Bid my anxious fears subside;
   Bear me thro' the swelling current,
   Land me safe on Canaan's side:
   Songs of praises,
   I will ever give to Thee.

No. 99. OLIVET.

1. My faith looks up to Thee,
   Thou Lamb of Calvary,
   Savior divine:
   Now hear me while I pray,
   Take all my guilt away,
   Oh, let me from this day
   Be wholly Thine.

2. May Thy rich grace impart
   Strength to my fainting heart,
   My zeal inspire;
   As Thou hast died for me,
   Oh, may my love to Thee
   Pure, warm and changeless be,
   A living fire!

3. While life's dark maze I tread,
   And griefs around me spread,
   Be Thou my guide;
   Bid darkness turn to day,
   Wipe sorrow's tears away,
   Nor let me ever stray
   From Thee aside.

No. 100. JESUS, THE LIFE-BOAT.

J. J. MAXFIELD. CHAS. H. GABRIEL.

1. I've looked my life o-ver and count-ed my store, And oh, what a tri-fle it seems! The life I have lived shall entice me no more, So full of un-re-al-ized dreams..... Since Je-sus, in mer-cy, has opened my eyes, My guilt-y con-di-tion I see,....... My spir-it with-
2. If one in ten thousand of all my life's sins Were brought into judgment with me,.... How should I con-fess all the vileness within To an-y, dear Sav-ior, but Thee?...... But since Thou art read-y and waiting to hear, Thy mercy I free-ly em-brace;..... O speak the glad
3. Too long I have wandered a-way from the fold, And gone where my fan-cy has led;...... Too long in-to bondage to sin I was sold To hun-ger and fam-ish for bread,...... But here at the cross, where I humble my soul, The blood has been sprinkled for me,...... And Thou, while the

COPYRIGHT, 1894, BY CHAS. H. GABRIEL.

Jesus, the Life-Boat.

No. 101. TRUSTING JESUS. HALLELUJAH!

HARRIET E. JONES.   D. B. TOWNER.

1. I am trust-ing in the Lord, Hal-le-lu-jah! I be-lieve His ev-'ry word. Hal-le-lu-jah! In the midst of ev-'ry ill, I will bow to His sweet will, Love, o-bey and trust Him still, Hal-le-lu-jah!
2. Midst the tem-pest I will sing, Hal-le-lu-jah! Ev-er trust-ing in my King. Hal-le-lu-jah! When the waves are ris-ing high, He, the help-er ev-er nigh, Sweet-ly whispers, "It is I." Hal-le-lu-jah!
3. With my eyes up-on the cross, Hal-le-lu-jah! I can bear the earth-ly loss. Hal-le-lu-jah! Sing His praise a-mid the pain, Who for me was scourged and slain, Sing it o'er and o'er a-gain, Hal-le-lu-jah!

CHORUS.

I am trust-ing, I am trust-ing, trusting, all a-long the wea-ry way, Hal-le-lu-jah! I am

COPYRIGHT, 1891, BY D. B. TOWNER.

Trusting Jesus. Hallelujah!

trust - ing, Hal - le - lu - jah! Sweet-ly trust-ing Je - sus day by day.

No. 102. ALL HAIL THE POWER.

E. PERRONET.   J. H. KURZENKNABE.

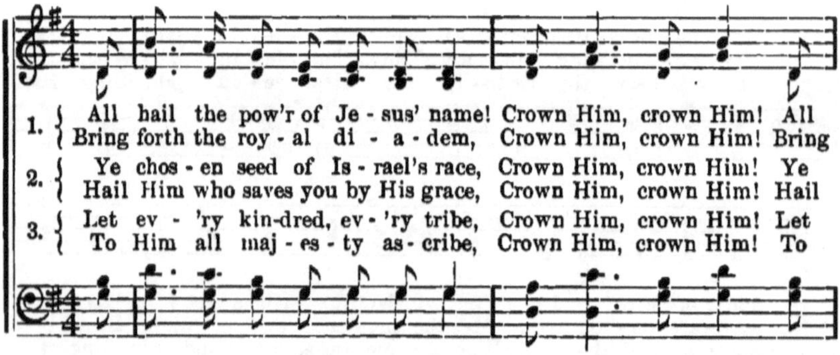

1. { All hail the pow'r of Je - sus' name! Crown Him, crown Him! All
    Bring forth the roy - al di - a - dem, Crown Him, crown Him! Bring
2. { Ye chos - en seed of Is - rael's race, Crown Him, crown Him! Ye
    Hail Him who saves you by His grace, Crown Him, crown Him! Hail
3. { Let ev - 'ry kin-dred, ev - 'ry tribe, Crown Him, crown Him! Let
    To Him all maj - es - ty as - cribe, Crown Him, crown Him! To

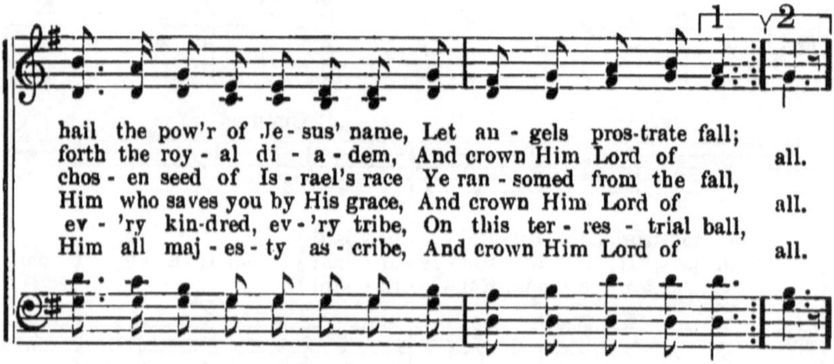

hail the pow'r of Je - sus' name, Let an - gels pros-trate fall;
forth the roy - al di - a - dem, And crown Him Lord of   all.
chos - en seed of Is - rael's race Ye ran - somed from the fall,
Him who saves you by His grace, And crown Him Lord of   all.
ev - 'ry kin-dred, ev - 'ry tribe, On this ter - res - trial ball,
Him all maj - es - ty as - cribe, And crown Him Lord of   all.

CHORUS.

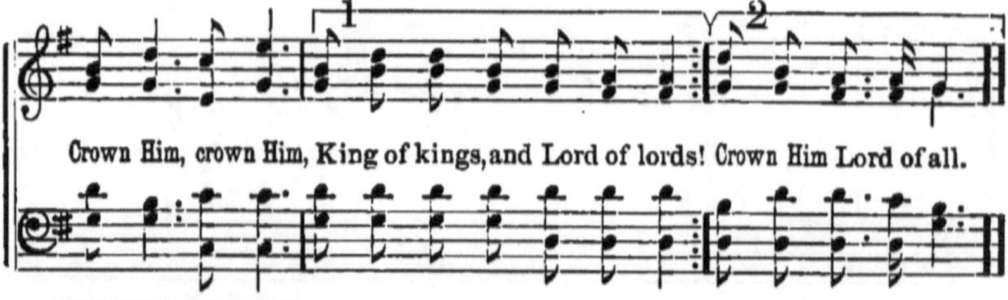

Crown Him, crown Him, King of kings, and Lord of lords! Crown Him Lord of all.

COPYRIGHT BY J. H. KURZENKNABE.

Seeking the Lost.

Into the fold of my Redeemer,
Into the fold........... of my Redeem - er,......

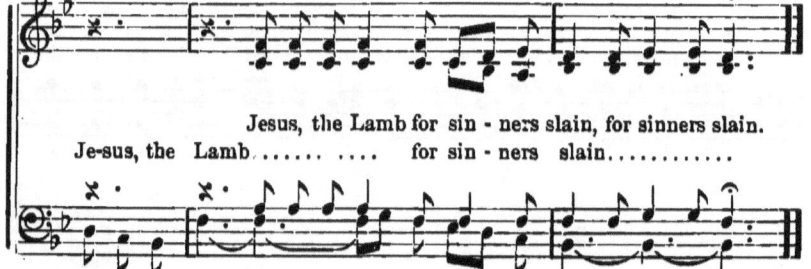

Jesus, the Lamb for sin - ners slain, for sinners slain.
Jesus, the Lamb........ .... for sin - ners slain............

No. 104. THE GREAT PHYSICIAN.

1 The great Physician now is here,
   The sympathizing Jesus;
He speaks the drooping heart to cheer,
   Oh, hear the voice of Jesus.

CHORUS.

Sweetest note in seraph song,
Sweetest name on mortal tongue,
Sweetest carol ever sung;
   Jesus, blessed Jesus.

2 Your many sins are all forgiven,
   Oh, hear the voice of Jesus;
Go on your way in peace to heaven,
   And wear a crown with Jesus.

3 All glory to the dying Lamb!
   I now believe in Jesus;
I love the blessed Savior's name,
   I love the name of Jesus.

No. 105. COME, YE SINNERS.

1 Come, ye sinners, poor and needy,
   Weak and wounded, sick and sore,
Jesus ready stands to save you,
   Full of pity, love, and power

CHORUS.

Turn to the Lord and seek salvation,
   Sound the praise of His dear name;
Glory, honor, and salvation,
   Christ the Lord has come to reign.

2 Now, ye needy, come and welcome,
   God's free bounty glorify;
True belief and true repentance,
   Every grace that brings you nigh.

3 Let not conscience make you linger,
   Nor of fitness fondly dream;
All the fitness He requireth,
   Is to feel your need of Him.

No. 106. HAVE YOU LEARNED TO PRAY.

Mrs. L. M. Beal Bateman.   C. D. Emerson.

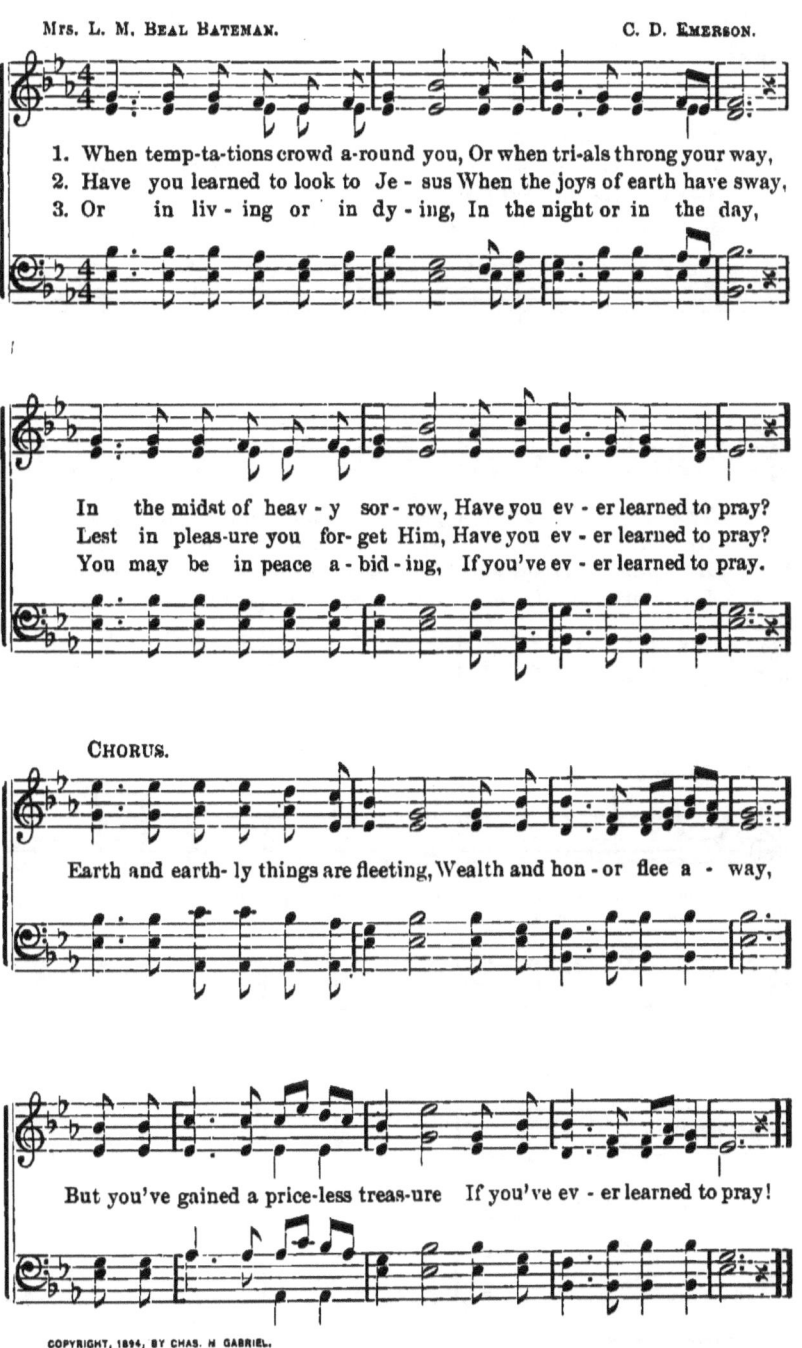

1. When temp-ta-tions crowd a-round you, Or when tri-als throng your way,
2. Have you learned to look to Je - sus When the joys of earth have sway,
3. Or in liv - ing or in dy - ing, In the night or in the day,

In the midst of heav - y sor - row, Have you ev - er learned to pray?
Lest in pleas-ure you for- get Him, Have you ev - er learned to pray?
You may be in peace a - bid - ing, If you've ev - er learned to pray.

CHORUS.

Earth and earth- ly things are fleeting, Wealth and hon - or flee a - way,

But you've gained a price-less treas-ure If you've ev - er learned to pray!

COPYRIGHT, 1894, BY CHAS. H GABRIEL.

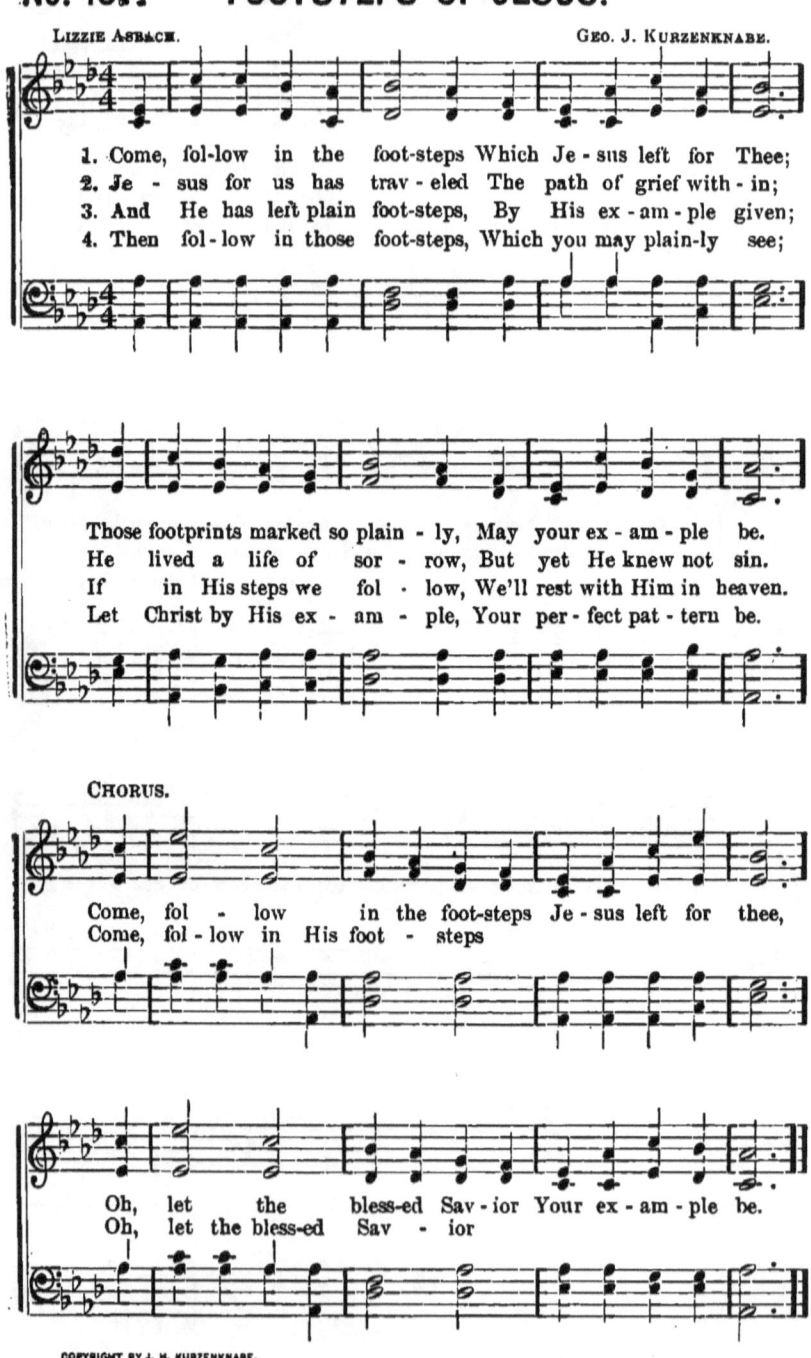

Will You Believe?

'Tis the sweet in-vit-ing mes-sage of a pre-cious Sav-ior's voice;

Will you now, all fear re-press-ing, Come and take the offered bless-ing?

While be-cause of your re-turn ing, All the hosts of heav'n re-joice.

No. 109. **COME TO JESUS.**

1. Come to Je-sus, Come to Je-sus, Come to Je-sus just now,
Just now come to Je-sus, Come to Je-sus just now.

2 He will save you.
3 Oh, believe Him.
4 He is able.
5 He is willing.
6 Call upon Him.
7 He will hear you.
8 Look unto Him.
9 He'll forgive you.
10 Only trust Him.
11 Jesus loves you.
12 Don't reject Him.
13 I believe Him.

Hear the Savior Calling.

Je - sus is wait - - - ing to save you to - day.
For Je - sus is wait-ing

No. 117.   TAKE ME AS I AM.
Rev. J. H. Stockton,

1. Je - sus, my Lord, to Thee I cry; Unless Thou help me, I must die;
2. Helpless I am, and full of guilt, But yet Thy blood for me was spilt;
3. No pre - par - a - tion can I make, My best resolves I on - ly break;
4. I thirst, I long to know Thy love, Thy full sal-va-tion I would prove;

FINE.

D.S.—Oh, bring Thy free sal - va-tion nigh, And take me as I am!
And Thou canst make me what Thou wilt, But take me as I am!
Yet save me for Thine own name's sake, And take me as I am!
But since to Thee I can - not move, Oh, take me as I am!

REFRAIN.   D. S.

Take me as I am,..... Take me as I am......
Take me, take me as I am, Take me, take me as I am.

5 If Thou hast work for me to do,
   Inspire my will, my heart renew,
   And work both in and by me, too,
     But take me as I am!

6 And when at last the work is done,
   The battle o'er, the vict'ry won,
   Still, still my cry shall be alone,
     Lord, take me as I am!

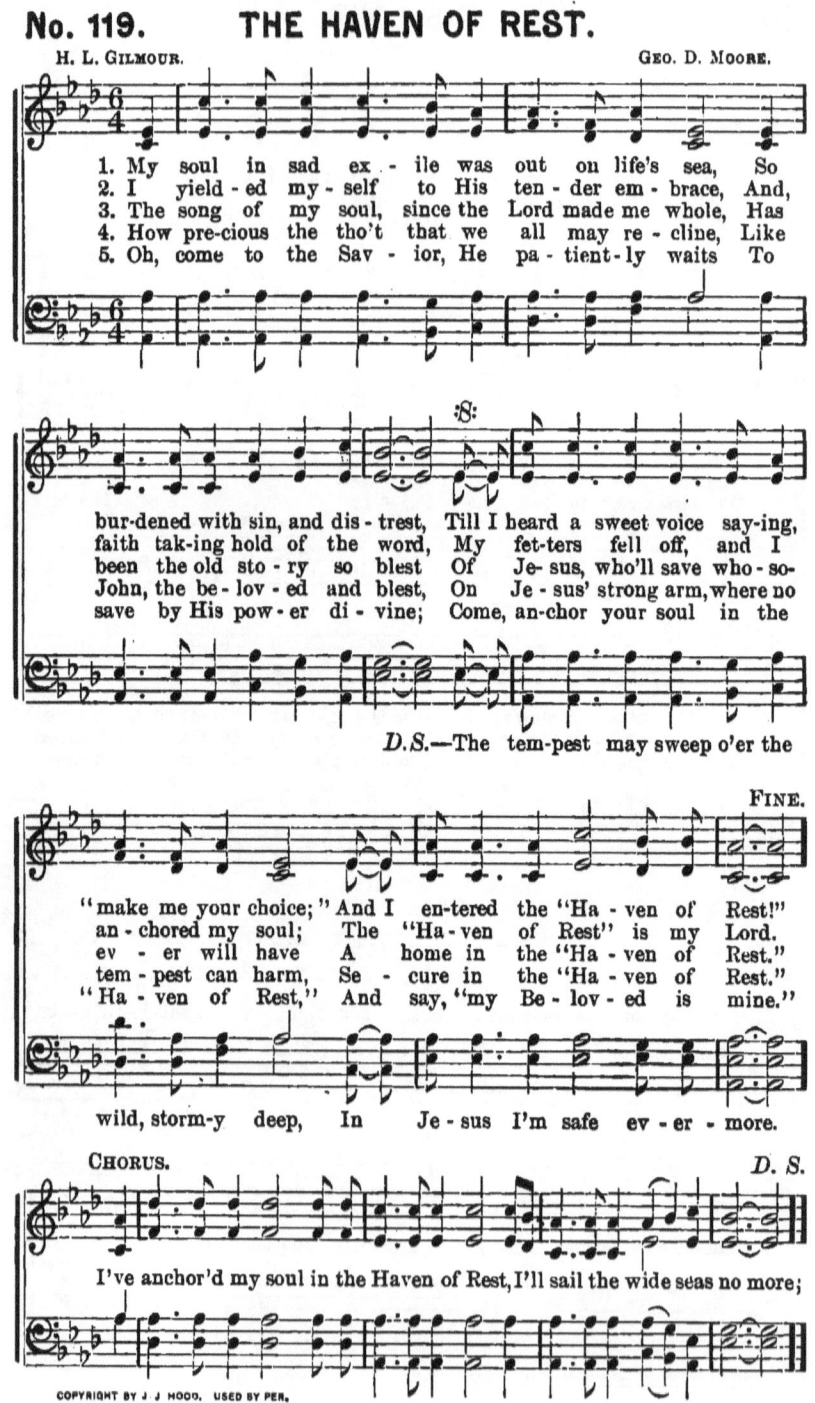

Marching to the Land Above.

beau-ti-ful land a-bove; To a land where dwells e-
beau-ti-ful cit - y fair; Where the an - gel au - thems
beau-ti-ful home of God; And our guide-book is His

ter - nal love, Beau-ti-ful land a - bove, land a - bove.
fill the air, Beau-ti-ful cit - y fair, cit - y fair.
ho - ly word, Beau-ti-ful word of God, word of God.

No. 125. BECAUSE HE LOVES US SO.

CHAS. E. NEAL.

1. { We love to sing of Je - sus; He does so much, we know,
   { To make us good and hap-py, [Omit. . . . .]
2. { We love to work for Je - sus, And ev - 'ry day to go
   { And do some lit - tle kind-ness, [Omit. . . . .]
3. { We love to pray to Je - sus, From whom all bless-ings flow;
   { And well we know He hears us, [Omit. . . . .]

CHORUS.

Because He loves us so. We'll love Him, we'll love Him, While in this

world below: And then He'll take us home to heav'n, Because He loves us so.

COPYRIGHT, 1893, BY CHAS. H. GABRIEL.

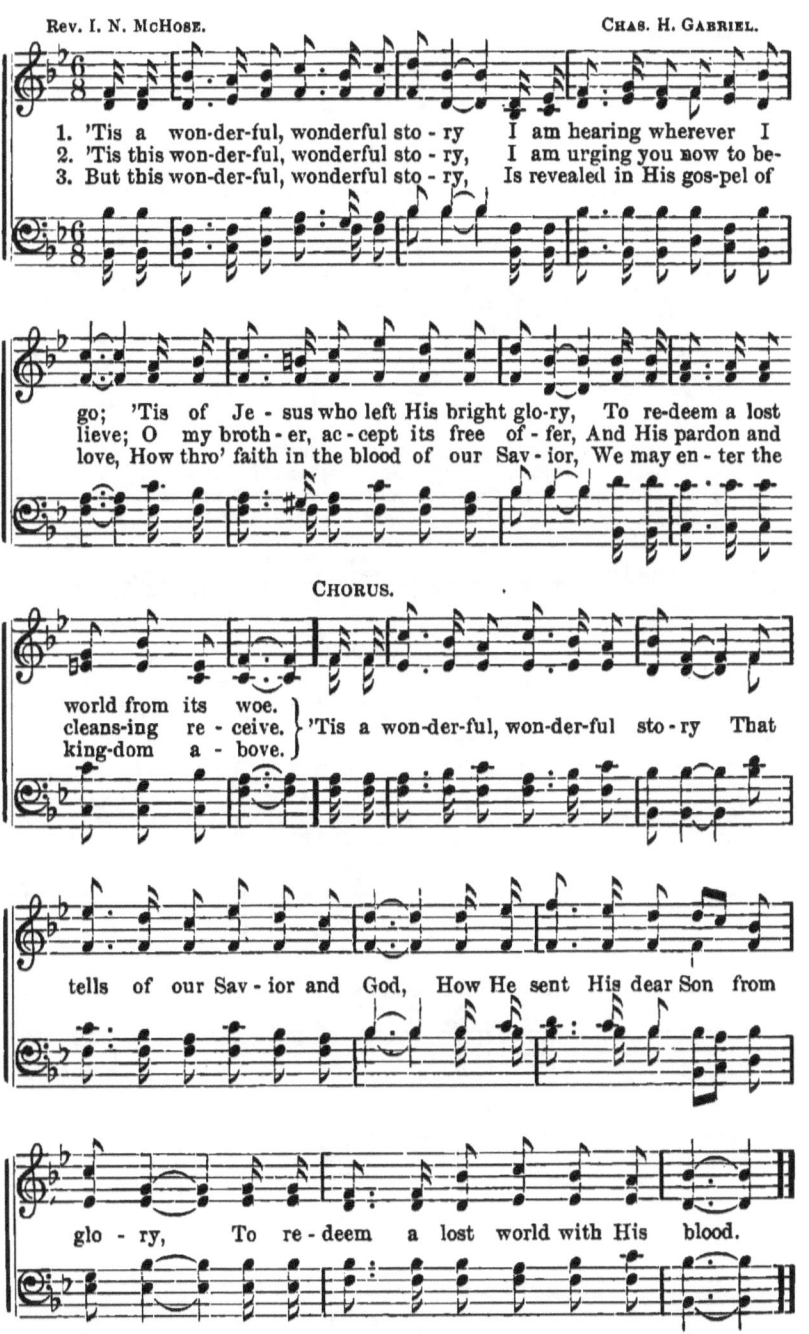

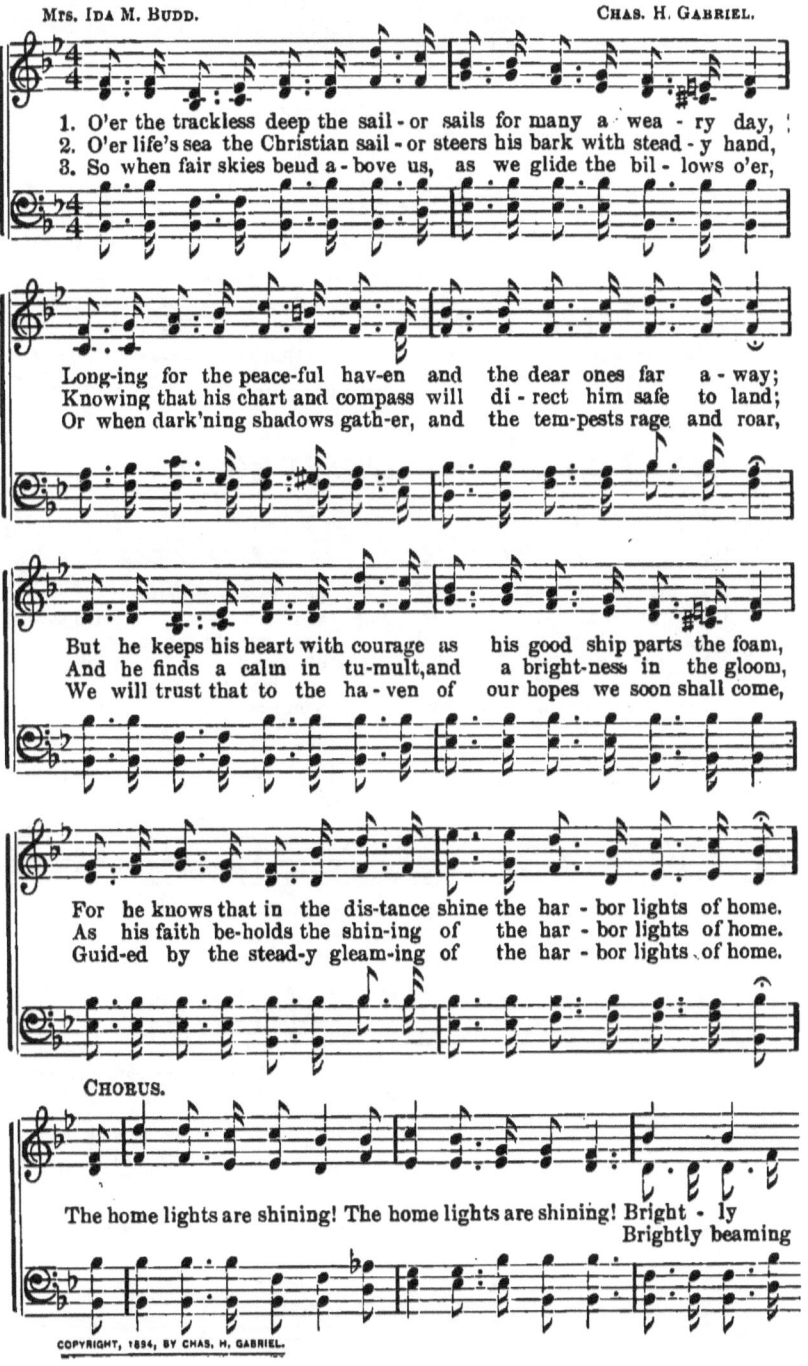

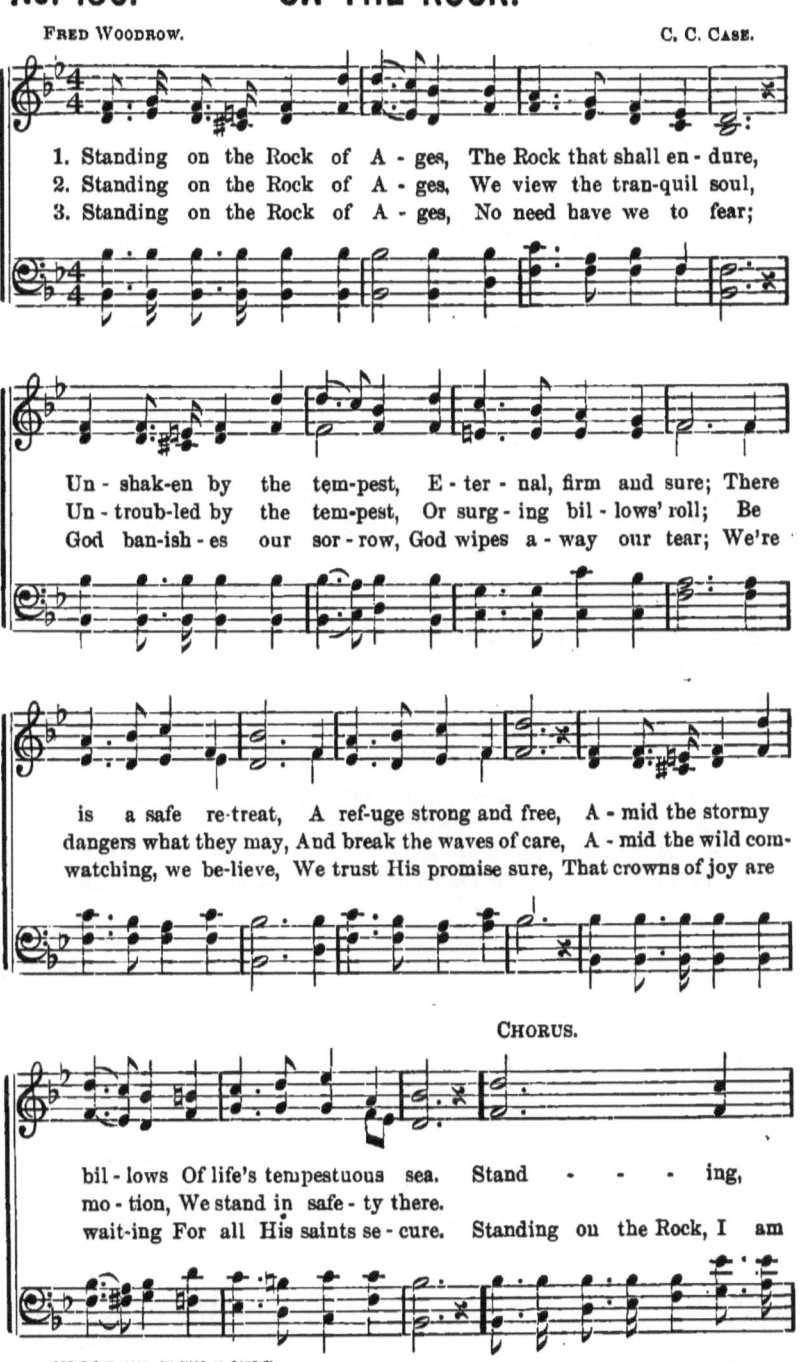

He is Able to Deliver Thee.

a - - - ble to de-liv-er thee; Tho' by sin op-prest,
a - ble, He is a - ble
Go to Him for rest, Our God is a - ble to de-liv-er thee.

No. 143. DENNIS.

JOHN FAWCETT. GEO. NAEGELI.

1. Blest be the tie that binds Our hearts in Chris-tian love; The
2. Be-fore our Fa-ther's throne, We pour our ar-dent prayers; Our
3. We share our mu-tual woes; Our mu-tual bur-dens bear; And
4. When we a-sun-der part, It gives us in-ward pain; But

fel-low-ship of kin-dred minds Is like to that a-bove.
fears, our hopes, our aims are one, Our com-forts and our cares.
oft-en for each oth-er flows, The sym-pa-thiz-ing tear.
we shall still be joined in heart, And hope to meet a-gain.

I am the Way.

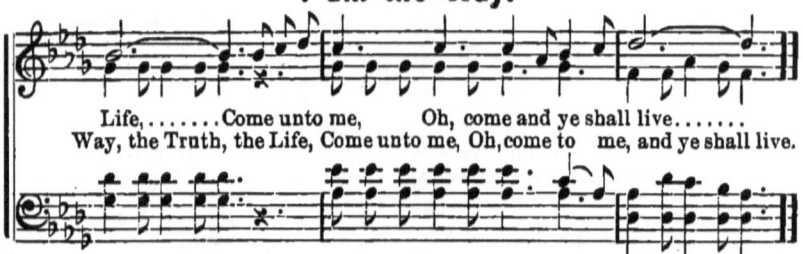

Life,......Come unto me, Oh, come and ye shall live.......
Way, the Truth, the Life, Come unto me, Oh, come to me, and ye shall live.

No. 145. BRINGING IN THE SHEAVES.

K. Shaw. Geo. A. Minor.

1 Sowing in the morning, sowing seeds of kindness,
  Sowing in the noontide, and the dewy eves;
  Waiting for the harvest, and the time of reaping,
  We shall come rejoicing, bringing in the sheaves.

Cho.—Bringing in the sheaves, bringing in the sheaves,
  We shall come rejoicing, bringing in the sheaves.

2 Sowing in the sunshine, sowing in the shadows,
  Fearing neither clouds nor winter's chilling breeze;
  By and by the harvest, and the labor ended,
  We shall come rejoicing, bringing in the sheaves.

3 Go then, ever weeping, sowing for the Master,
  Though the loss sustained our spirit often grieves;
  When our weeping's over, He will bid us welcome,
  We shall come rejoicing, bringing in the sheaves.

The Sheltering Cross.

And sheltered here,............ I will a-bide............
And sheltered here, I will a-bide.

No. 149. PRAISE HIM.

J. KEMPTHORN.   H. A. HENRY.

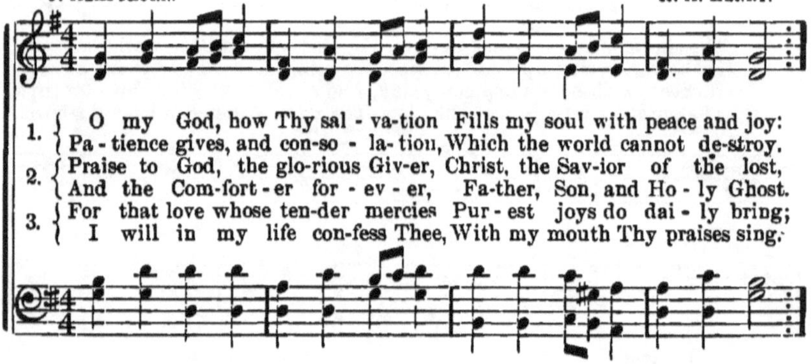

1. O my God, how Thy sal-va-tion Fills my soul with peace and joy:
   Pa-tience gives, and con-so-la-tion, Which the world cannot de-stroy.
2. Praise to God, the glo-rious Giv-er, Christ, the Sav-ior of the lost,
   And the Com-fort-er for-ev-er, Fa-ther, Son, and Ho-ly Ghost.
3. For that love whose ten-der mercies Pur-est joys do dai-ly bring;
   I will in my life con-fess Thee, With my mouth Thy praises sing.

CHORUS.

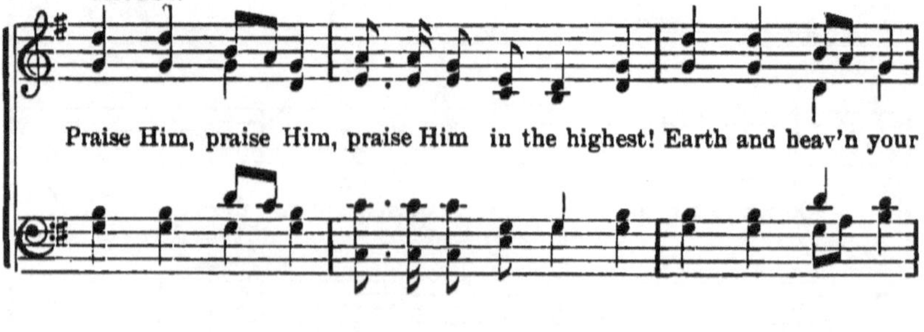

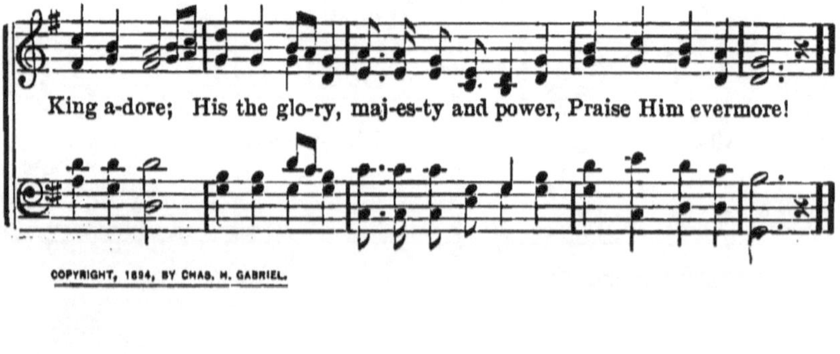

Praise Him, praise Him, praise Him in the highest! Earth and heav'n your King a-dore; His the glo-ry, maj-es-ty and power, Praise Him evermore!

COPYRIGHT, 1894, BY CHAS. H. GABRIEL.

Praying for You.

No. 152.   **OUR FATHERS' GOD.**

Fred Woodrow.   E. S. Lorenz.

1. Our Fa-thers trust-ed in the Lord, He was their ref-uge strong;
2. For faith and truth and love of God, They fought the ho-ly fight;
3. They, one by one, have cross'd the flood, And reached the Canaan shore;

Their com-fort-er in gloom-y days, Their suc-cor and their song.
The sen-ti-nels of Zi-on's walls, And watch-ers in the night.
And, one by one, we fol-low on To those who've gone be-fore.

CHORUS.

For Him they lived,—for Him they died, And con-quer-ors they came

Thro' storm-y flood and mar-tyr fire, To glo-ri-fy His name.

Copyright, 1891, by Chas. H. Gabriel.

No. 153. OH, SUCH WONDERFUL LOVE.

BY PER. HENRY DATE, OWNER OF COPYRIGHT.

Steadily Marching On.

CHORUS.

Steadily marching on With our banner waving o'er us, Steadily marching on, while we sing the joy-ful cho-rus; Stead-i-ly marching on, pil-lar and cloud go-ing be-fore us, To the realms of glo-ry, to our home on high.

No. 156.   THE LORD'S PRAYER.

GREGORIAN.

1 Our Father which art in heaven, | Hallowed | be Thy | name.‖
   Thy kingdom come. Thy will be done in | earth, as it | is in | heaven.
2 Give us this | day our— | daily | bread.‖
   And forgive us our debts, as | we for- | give our | debtors.
3 And lead us not into temptation, but de- | liver | us from | evil:‖
   For Thine is the kingdom, and the power, and the glory, for- | ever. | A-|men.

No. 159. THE WARNING CALL.

Words and Melody furnished by ISAAC NAYLOR.

1. Hark, sinner! list to the voice of the Lord! Jus-tice is standing with up-lift-ed sword: Mer-cy is plead-ing in path-os so sweet, Lay thy sins at Im-man-u-el's feet.
2. Down in the rap-ids of sin, shame and blight, Thou'rt be-ing hur-ried to darkness and night; Stop ere thou ends in the whirlpool of woe, Where the God-less and pen-i-tentless go.
3. Swift-ly the cur-rent of sin bears thee on! Look, sin-ner, look to the cru-ci-fied One: Hark! hear His voice saying; "Come unto me," Come, oh, come, and thy soul shall be free.
4. List-en, oh, list-en,—give ear to the call; Come, for He call-eth the rich, poor, and all! Jesus stands waiting with arms open wide, Come! there's ref-uge in His riv-en side.

Rit. e dim.

CHORUS.

Hark! Je-sus calls thee to-day,........ Come, and no long-er de-lay........ Poor, blind, dis-
Im-man-u-el's feet, Je-sus calls thee today, no longer de-lay.

COPYRIGHT, 1896 BY CHAS. H. GABRIEL.

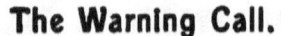

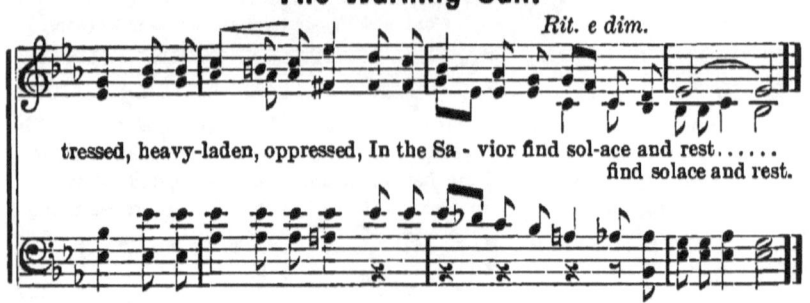

The Warning Call.

Rit. e dim.
tressed, heavy-laden, oppressed, In the Sa - vior find sol-ace and rest......
find solace and rest.

No. 160. CORONATION.

Rev. E. Perronet. O. Holden.

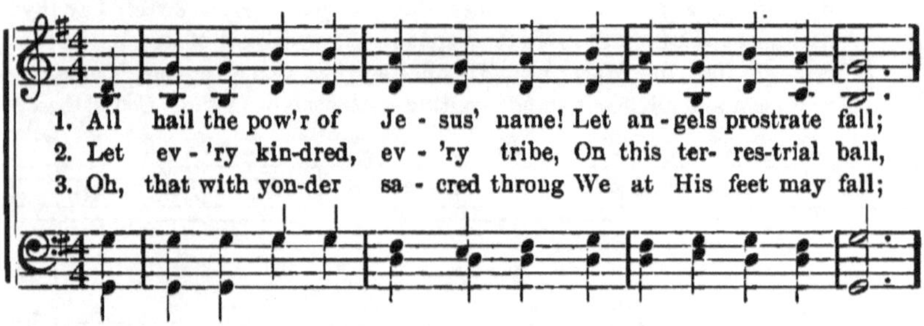

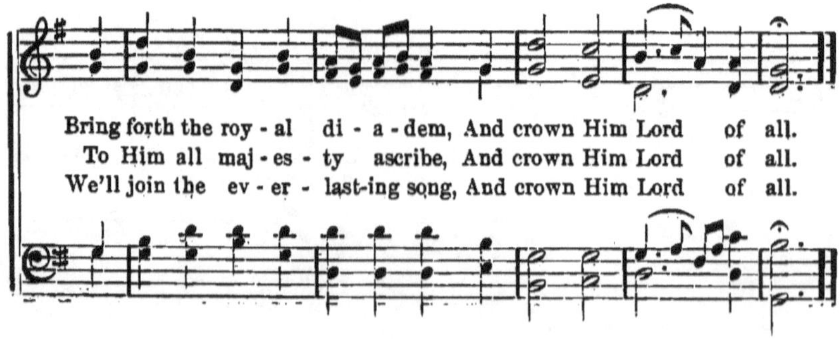

1. All hail the pow'r of Je - sus' name! Let an-gels prostrate fall;
2. Let ev - 'ry kin-dred, ev - 'ry tribe, On this ter- res-trial ball,
3. Oh, that with yon-der sa - cred throng We at His feet may fall;

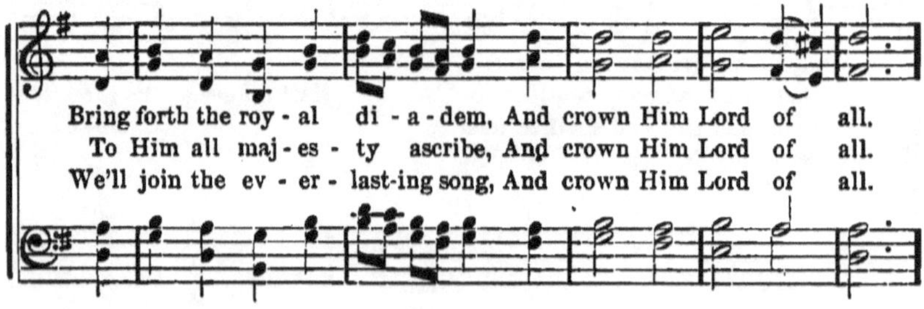

Bring forth the roy - al di - a - dem, And crown Him Lord of all.
To Him all maj - es - ty ascribe, And crown Him Lord of all.
We'll join the ev - er - last-ing song, And crown Him Lord of all.

Bring forth the roy - al di - a - dem, And crown Him Lord of all.
To Him all maj - es - ty ascribe, And crown Him Lord of all.
We'll join the ev - er - last-ing song, And crown Him Lord of all.

Sailing O'er the Ocean.

Christ,............ our Pi-lot, stands at the wheel,
Christ, our trust-y Pi - lot, Christ, our Pi-lot, stands at the wheel,

Hal - le - - lu - jah! we are go - ing home.
Hal - le - lu - jah! hal - le - lu - jah! we are go - ing home.

No. 164.   THERE IS A FOUNTAIN.

WILLIAM COWPER.   Western Melody.

1. { There is a fountain filled with blood, Drawn from Immanuel's veins,
    And sin-ners plunged beneath that flood, [Omit ....]

Lose all their guilty stains. Lose all their guilty stains, Lose all their guilty stains.

2 The dying thief rejoiced to see
  That fountain in his day;
  And there may I though vile as he,
  Wash all my sins away.

3 Dear dying Lamb! Thy precious blood
  Shall never lose its power,
  Till all the ransomed Church of God
  Are saved to sin no more.

4 E'er since by faith, I saw the stream
  Thy flowing wounds supply,
  Redeeming love has been my theme,
  And shall be, till I die.

5 Then in a nobler, sweeter song,
  I'll sing Thy power to save,
  When this poor lisping, stamm'ring
  Lies silent in the grave. [tongue,

No. 169. HE HATH REDEEMED ME.

IDA M. BUDD.   CHAS. H. GABRIEL.

1. Christ is my Sav-ior; He hath redeemed me, Sealed my forgiveness and called me His friend; Un-to my heart He is ten-der-ly say-ing:
2. When I in darkness aim-less-ly wandered, Bound by the fet-ters of er-ror and sin; Faith-ful He sought me, so earn-est-ly plead-ing,
3. Slow-ly my heart its stubborn will yield-ed, Slow-ly un-closed to His pres-ence di-vine, But He hath conquered, and gladly I own Him;
4. He hath redeemed me! Lost one, O lost one; Still He is seek-ing the err-ing to win; At your heart's door He is knocking and wait-ing,

"Lo! I am with you, e'en un-to the end!"
Pa-tient-ly call-ing the wan-der-er in.
Praise His dear name, His sal-va-tion is mine!
Will you not hear Him, and bid Him come in?

CHORUS.

He hath redeemed me! He hath redeemed me! Glo-ry and praise be unto His name! Kind His com-passion and tender His pit-y, Yes-ter-day, now, and for-ev-er the same!

COPYRIGHT, 1894, BY CHAS. H. GABRIEL.

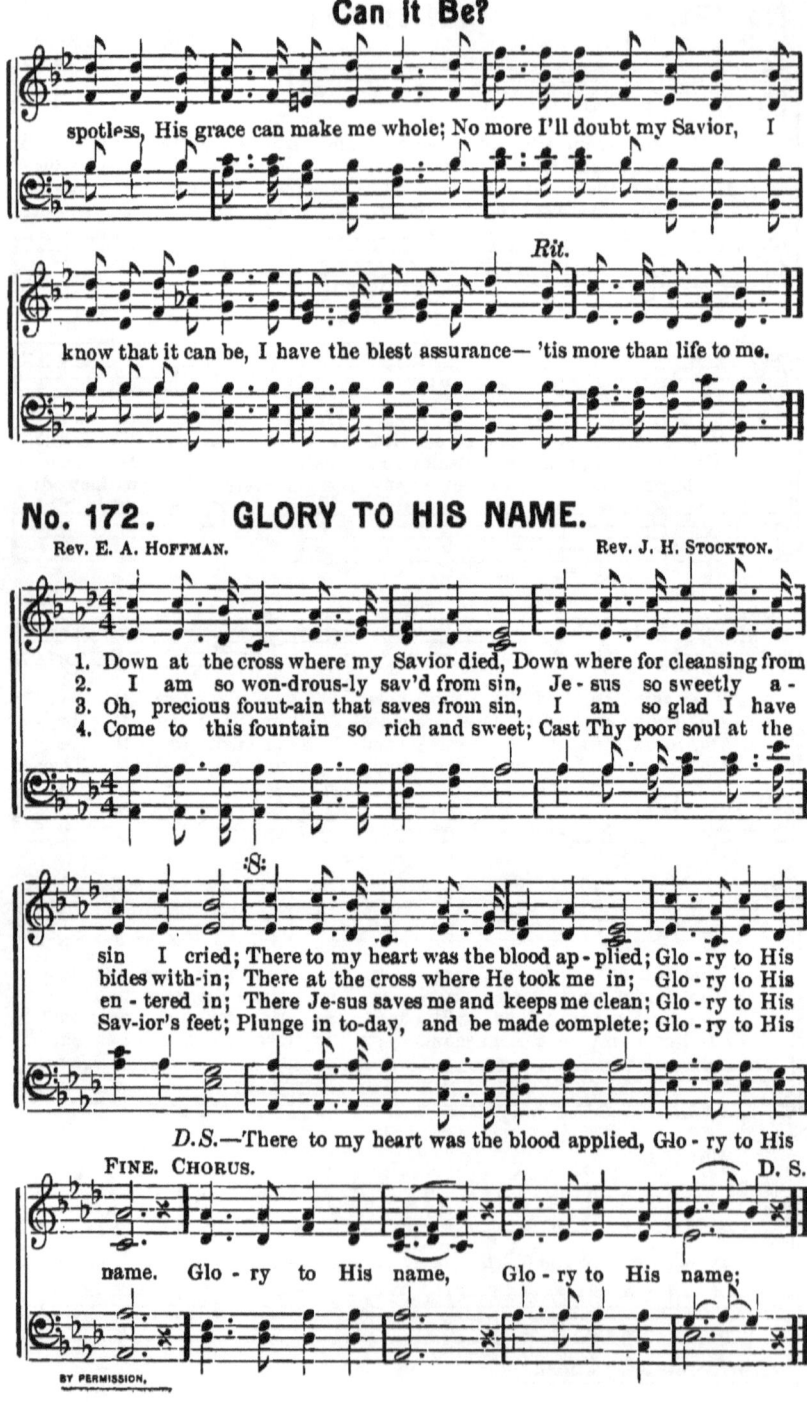

Joy Among the Angels.

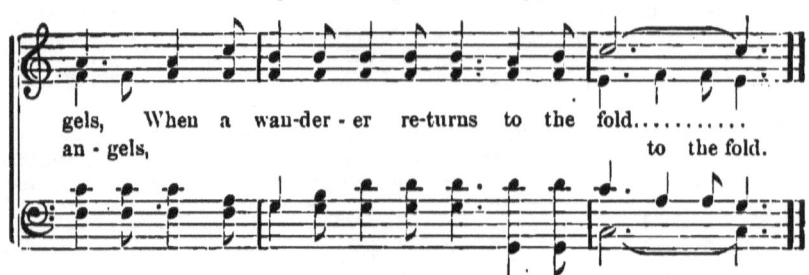

gels, When a wan-der-er re-turns to the fold..........
an-gels, to the fold.

No. 174. MORE LOVE TO THEE, O CHRIST.

Mrs. E. Prentiss.   Dr. W. H. Doane.

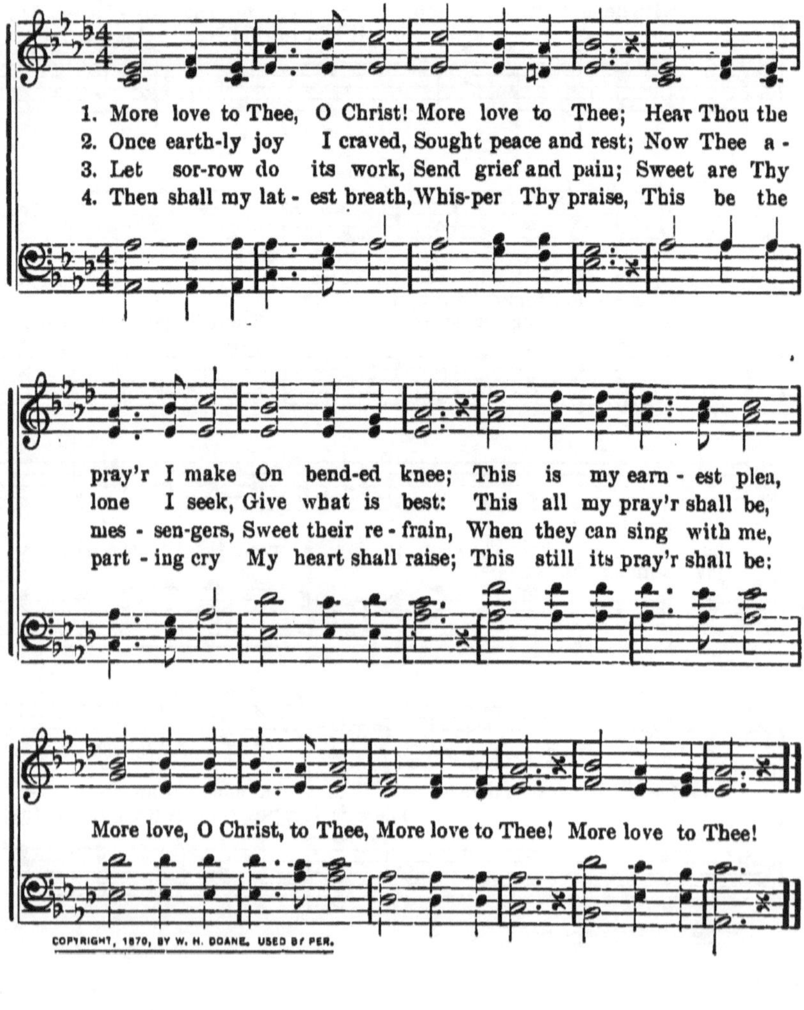

1. More love to Thee, O Christ! More love to Thee; Hear Thou the
2. Once earth-ly joy I craved, Sought peace and rest; Now Thee a-
3. Let sor-row do its work, Send grief and pain; Sweet are Thy
4. Then shall my lat-est breath, Whis-per Thy praise, This be the

pray'r I make On bend-ed knee; This is my earn-est plea,
lone I seek, Give what is best: This all my pray'r shall be,
mes-sen-gers, Sweet their re-frain, When they can sing with me,
part-ing cry My heart shall raise; This still its pray'r shall be:

More love, O Christ, to Thee, More love to Thee! More love to Thee!

COPYRIGHT, 1870, BY W. H. DOANE. USED BY PER.

No. 175. STEER TOWARD THE LIGHT.

GERTRUDE T. CLARK.   W. A. OGDEN.

1. Fierce is the tem-pest, loud is its roar, Storm-tossed the mar-in-er, far from the shore; See! what is put-ting the dark-ness to flight? Je-sus, the Morning Star; steer t'ward the light!
2. Storms cannot hide it, years can-not fade; Firm its foun-da-tion is, be not a-fraid; Heav'n's ample har-bor shall soon greet thy sight, Watch for the dawn of day, steer t'ward the light!
3. When wild the tem-pest round thee is hurled, Look un-to Je-sus, the hope of the world; Bright shall the day be that fol-lows the night, Cour-age, then, mar-in-er, steer t'ward the light!

CHORUS.

Brightly it gleams, and its pure sil-ver beams Scat-ter the gloom of the night, of the night; Tho' the storms round thee rave, He is mighty to save, Then, mariner, steer t'ward the light.

COPYRIGHT, 1893, BY CHAS. H. GABRIEL.

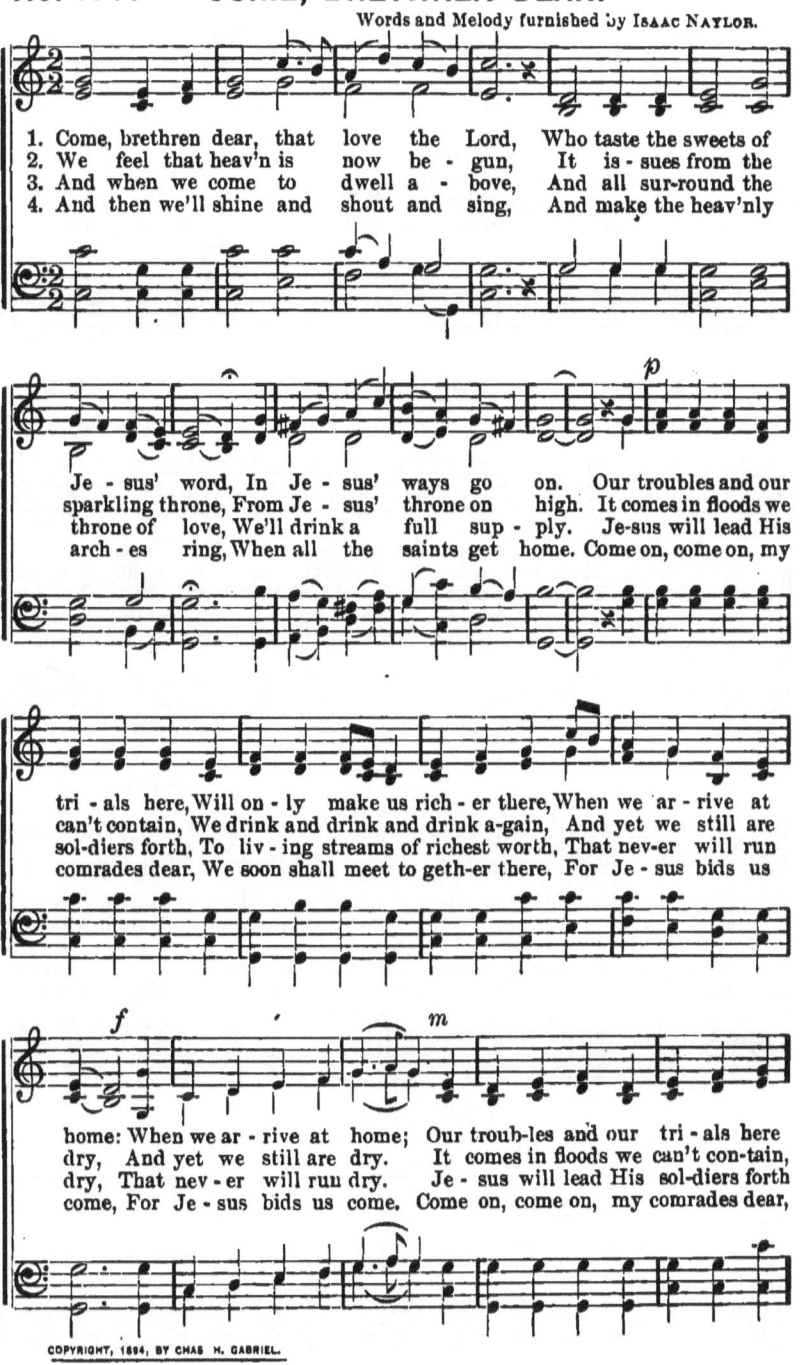

No. 179. "THEY SHALL BE MINE."

IDA SCOTT TAYLOR.   CHAS. H. GABRIEL.

1. They shall be mine, the jew-els I love, Shin-ing to grace
2. Kept from the world all spot-less with-in, Washed in the blood
3. They shall be mine, the sheep of my Fold—Walk-ing the streets

my king-dom a-bove; They shall be mine, When I shall ap-pear,
that cleanseth from sin, Bright as the stars that bril-liant-ly shine,
of glit-ter-ing gold, Sheltered and safe from sor-row and care,

CHORUS.

Gath-'ring my gems all price-less and clear.
Guard-ed from ill, oh, they shall be mine! } Com-ing, com-ing,
Gath-ered for Christ, all fade-less and fair.

some bright day; Let our hearts pre-pare the way! Je-sus

shall to earth come down, Gath-er-ing jew-els for His crown.

COPYRIGHT, 1894, BY CHAS. H. GABRIEL.

I'm Always Safe with Christ.

the King di - vine,...... .... En-fold - ed by His lov-ing care,
the King di-vine,

I'm safe with Christ,.............. no matter where..........
I'm safe with Christ, no matter where.

No. 182. HAPPY DAY.

P. DODDRIDGE.   E. F. RIMBAULT.

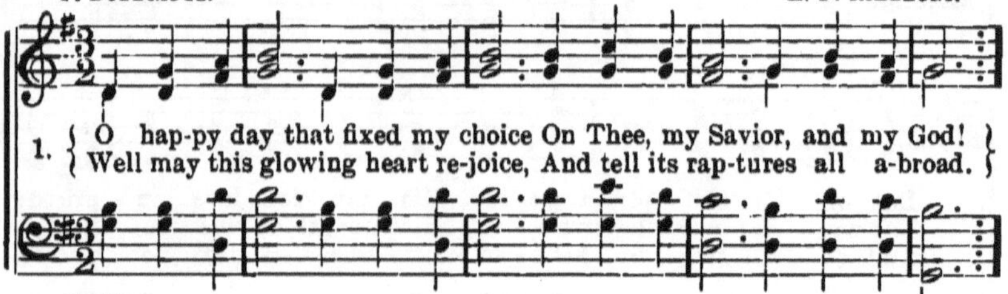

1. O hap-py day that fixed my choice On Thee, my Savior, and my God!
   Well may this glowing heart re-joice, And tell its rap-tures all a-broad.

CHORUS.   FINE.

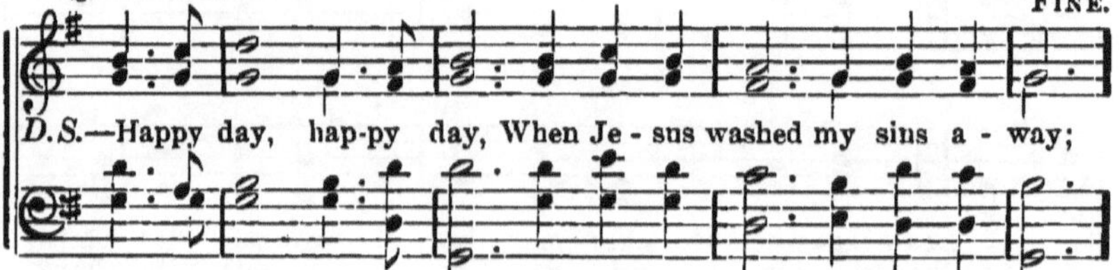

D.S.—Happy day, hap-py day, When Je - sus washed my sins a - way;

D. S.

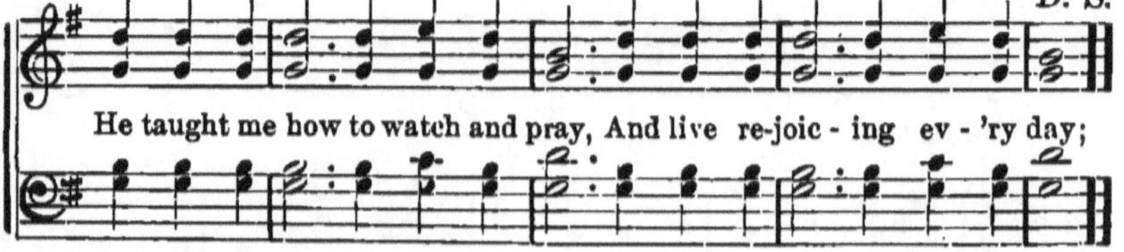

He taught me how to watch and pray, And live re-joic - ing ev - 'ry day;

2 O happy bond that seals my vows
   To Him who merits all my love;
 Let cheerful anthems fill His house,
   While to that sacred shrine I move.

3 'Tis done, the great transaction's done;
   I am my Lord's and He is mine;
 He drew me, and I follow'd on,
   Charm'd to confess the voice divine.

4 Now rest, my long-divided heart,
   Fixed on this blissful center, rest;
 Nor ever from thy Lord depart,
   With Him of every good possess'd.

5 High heav'n, that heard the solemn vow,
   That vow renew'd shall daily hear,
 Till in life's latest hour I bow,
   And bless in death a bond so dear.

No. 183. IT WILL NEVER GROW OLD.

Rev. W. W. Baily.   I. N. McHose.

1. Oh, have you not heard of that coun-try a - bove, The name of its King, and His in - fin - ite love? His chil - dren are death-less and hap - py, I'm told; Oh, will it a - bide, will it nev-er grow old?
2. That won-der-ful land has a cit - y of life, Ne'er darken'd with an - guish, nor dy - ing, nor strife; Its tem - ples and streets all are flash-ing with gold, Oh, can it be true, it will nev-er grow old?
3. A man-sion of won-der - ful beau-ty is there, And Je - sus that man - sion has gone to pre-pare; Its bright jas - per walls how I long to be - hold, And join in the song that will nev-er grow old.
4. They tell me its friendships and love are so pure, Its joys nev - er die, and its treas-ures are sure; And loved ones, de-part - ed, so si - lent and cold, Will greet us a-gain where we'll nev-er grow old.

D.S.—joy that's un-told, To think of that land that will nev-er grow old.

CHORUS.

'Twill al - ways be new, it will nev - er de - cay; No night ev - er comes, it will al - ways be day; It glad-dens my heart with a

BY PERMISSION.

A Great Glad Day.

CHORUS.

Oh, courage, heart,......press on, press on!.........For thee a
Oh, courage, heart,; press on, press on!

great glad day shall dawn,— A day of peace........
For thee a great glad day shall dawn, shall dawn,— A day of peace

and rest sub-lime,........'Twill come at last.......some-time, some-time.
and rest sublime, 'Twill come at last

No. 186. OH, TELL ME NO MORE.

Tune:—LYONS. Key of A.

1 Oh, tell me no more of this world's vain store,
   The time for such trifles with me now is o'er;
   A country I've found where true joys abound,
   To dwell I'm determined on that happy ground.

2 The souls that believe in paradise live,
   And me in that number will Jesus receive:
   My soul, don't delay; he calls thee away;
   Rise, follow thy Savior, and bless the glad day.

3 No mortal doth know what He can bestow,
   What light, strength, and comfort—go after Him, go;
   Lo, onward I move to a city above,
   None guesses how wondrous my journey will prove.

4 Great spoils I shall win from death, hell and sin,
   'Midst outward afflictions shall feel Christ within:
   And when I'm to die, "Receive me," I'll cry,
   For Jesus hath loved me, I cannot tell why:

5 But this I do find, we two are so joined,
   He'll not live in glory and leave me behind:
   So this is the race I'm running through grace,
   Henceforth, till admitted to see my Lord's face.

6 And now I'm in care my neighbors may share
   These blessings. to seek them will none of you dare?
   In bondage, Oh, why, and death will you lie,
   When one here assures you free grace is so nigh?

Sound It Out With Singing.

Joy and glad-ness bring-ing, If you know...... a Sav-ior's
If you know
love, Sound it out with sing-ing.
A Sav-ior's love, Sound it out

No. 188. I AM TRUSTING, LORD, IN THEE.

Rev. WM. McDonald. WM. G. Fischer.

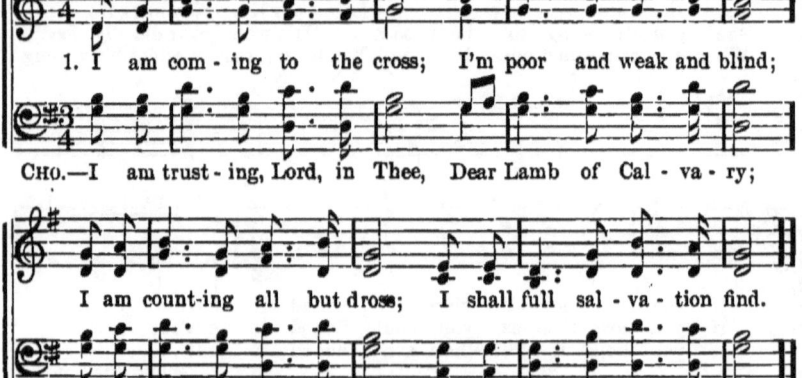

1. I am com-ing to the cross; I'm poor and weak and blind;
Cho.—I am trust-ing, Lord, in Thee, Dear Lamb of Cal-va-ry;

I am count-ing all but dross; I shall full sal-va-tion find.
Humbly at Thy cross I bow; Save me, Je-sus, save me now.

2 Long my heart has sighed for Thee;
   Long has evil dwelt within;
Jesus sweetly speaks to me,
   I will cleanse you from all sin.

3 Here I give my all to Thee,—
   Friends and time and earthly store,
Soul and body Thine to be—
   Wholly Thine—forevermore.

4 In the promises I trust;
   In the cleansing blood confide;

I am prostrate in the dust;
   I with Christ am crucified.

5 Jesus comes! He fills my soul!
   Perfected in love I am;
I am every whit made whole;
   Glory, glory to the Lamb!
     (Chorus to 5th verse.)
Still I'm trusting, Lord, in Thee,
   Dear Lamb of Calvary;
Humbly at Thy cross I bow—
   Jesus saves me! saves me now.

BY PERMISSION.

No. 189. IN THE BY AND BY.

Mrs. Ida M. Budd. Chas. H. Gabriel.

1. There will be sing-ing and great re-joic-ing Yon-der in glo-ry,
2. There will be wail-ing, sad lam-en-ta-tions, Bit-ter-est weep-ing,
3. In heav-en's mor-row shall we be chanting Praise and thanksgiving,
4. Grant us, O Fa-ther, that not with sad-ness Our souls shall meet Thee,

by and by; Sweet anthems ringing, in gladness voicing Salvation's sweet
by and by; Grief un-a-vail-ing, vain sup-pli-ca-tion, And sorrowful
by and by? Or, in our sor-row, be there la-ment-ing Our prod-i-gal
by and by, But let us, rath-er, with joy and gladness Haste onward to

Refrain.

sto-ry, by and by.   By and by,...... By and by,..... Singing and
reaping, by and by.   Weeping and
liv-ing, by and by?   Gladness and
greet Thee by and by.   By and by,   by and by, Our souls shall

praising by and by;...... Sing-ing and praising by and by;......
wail-ing by and by;...... Weep-ing and wail-ing by and by;......
sor-row by and by;....... Gladness and sor-row by and by;......
meet Thee, by and by, by and by; Our souls shall meet Thee, by and by, by and by.

Copyright, 1894, by Chas. H. Gabriel.

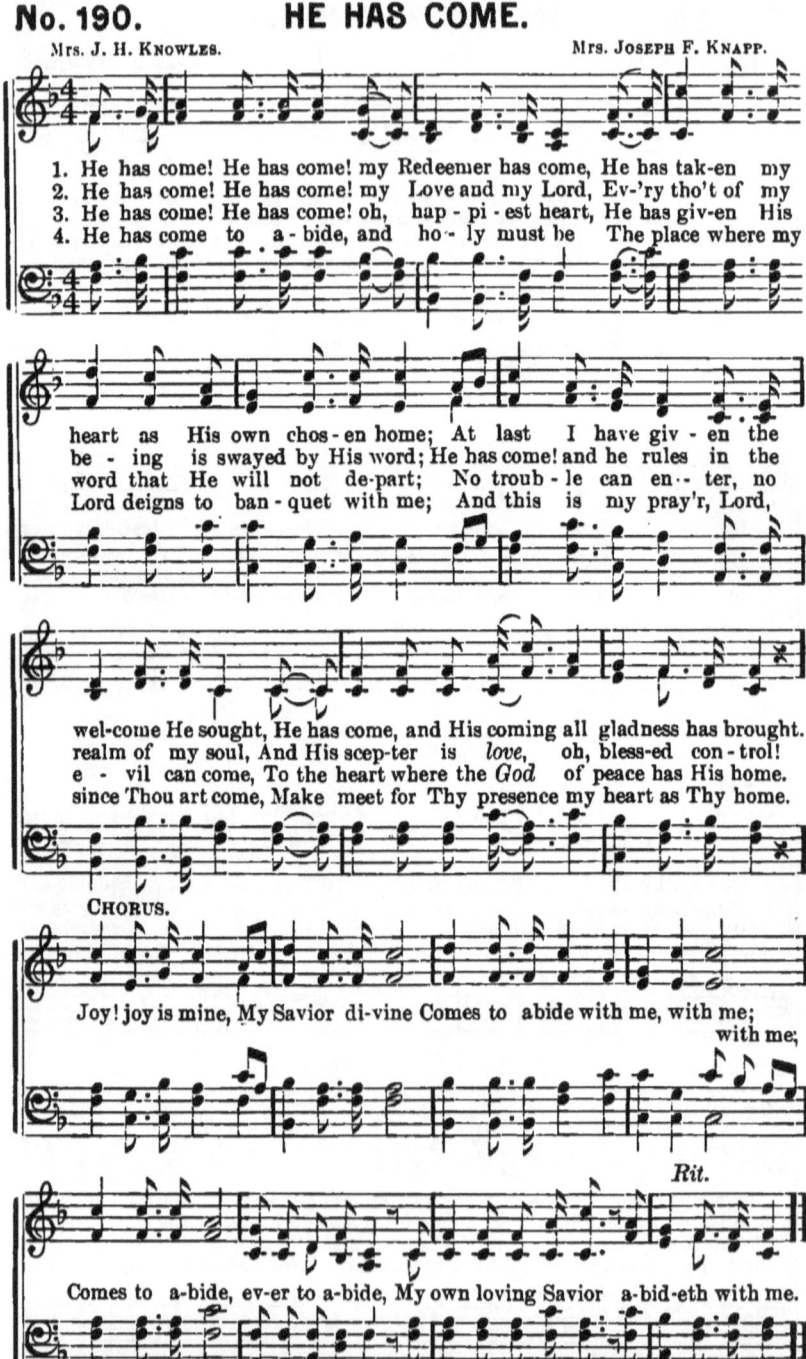

No More Wandering Sheep.

fold;............ No more in paths............ for-bid-den
wan-der from the fold; No more in paths
roam,........But find my joy with Thee at home........
forbidden roam, But find my joy and rest with Thee at home.

No. 192 THE MASTER COMES.

Rev. E. Gough. B. A. J. Newsome.

1. The Master comes, make straight His way! Let no vile passion say Him nay;
2. The Master comes! bring ointment meet, And crown His head with odors sweet;

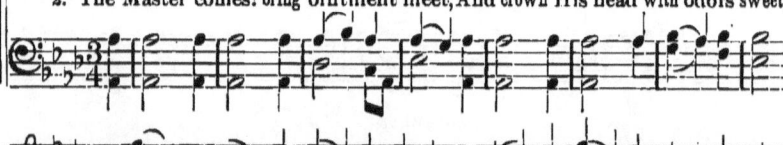

He comes to rid thee of thy sin,—O-pen thy heart and let Him in.
A ban-quet for thy King pre-pare, Let ev-'ry grace be stationed there.

3
Give Peace her dove, give Praise her lyre,
Bid languid Love stir up her fire,
While Zeal stands ready to fulfill
Each counsel of the Savior's will.

4
The Master comes! search well Thy heart,
Bid Satan from the shrine depart;
Break down the idols prized so long,
Write a new coronation song.

5
The Master comes! O happy thou!
Before thy gates He standeth now;
From other works awhile forbear,—
To welcome Christ be all thy care.

6
The Master comes! His face we see;
O Jesus, we have longed for Thee;
Into our hearts Thy fulness bring,
And make us like Thee while we sing.

COPYRIGHT, 1894, BY CHAS. H. GABRIEL.

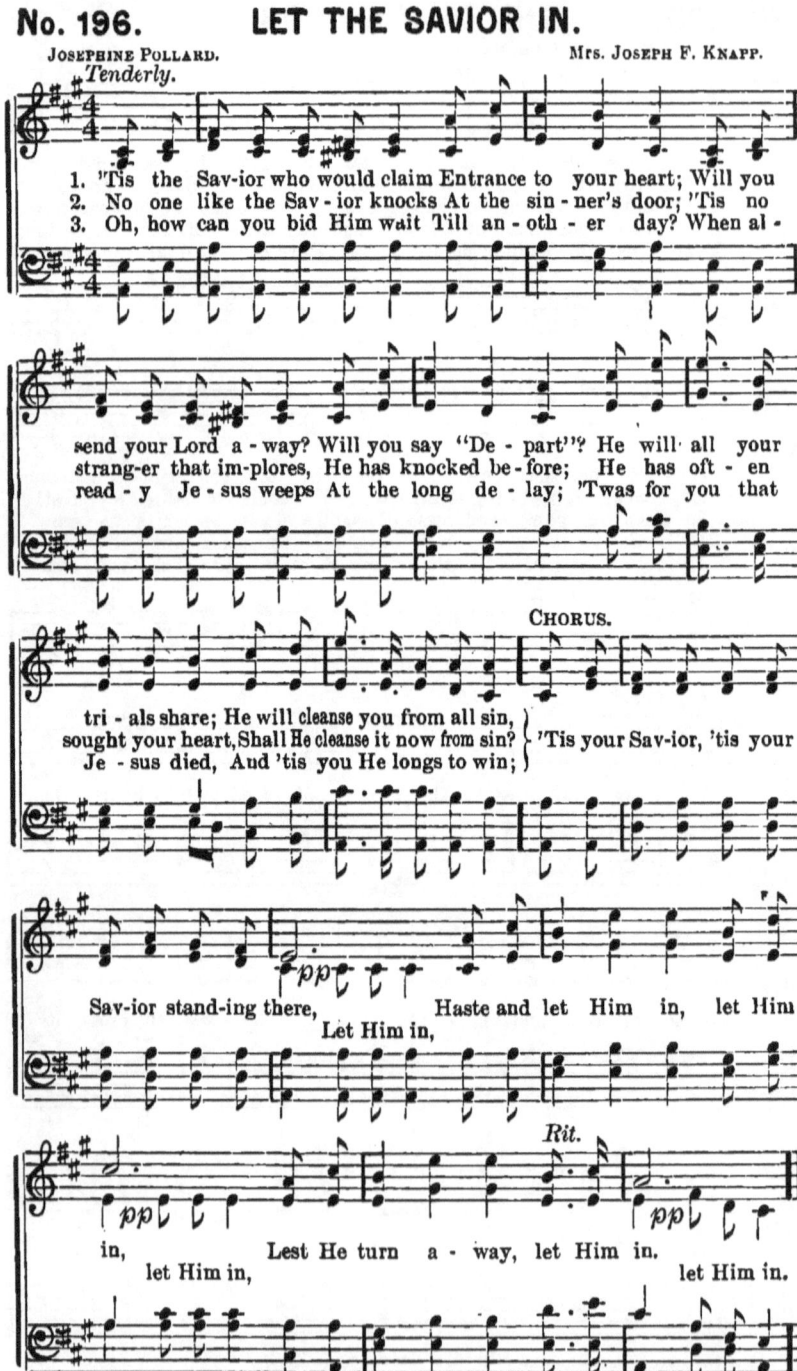

Scattering Precious Seed.

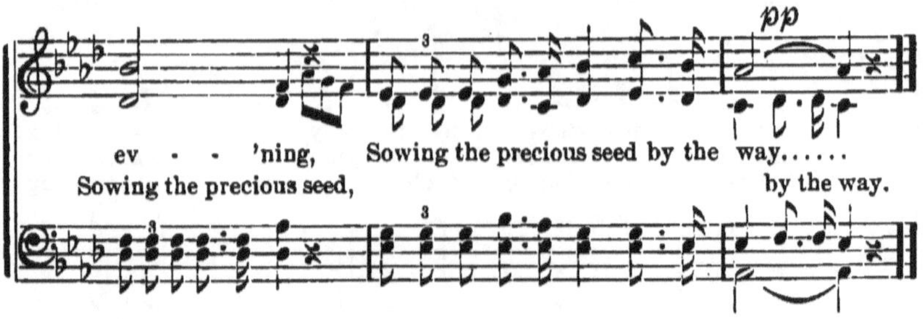

ev - - 'ning, Sowing the precious seed by the way......
Sowing the precious seed, by the way.

No. 198. WHO AT MY DOOR IS STANDING?

Mrs. M. B. C. Slade.   Dr. A. B. Everett.

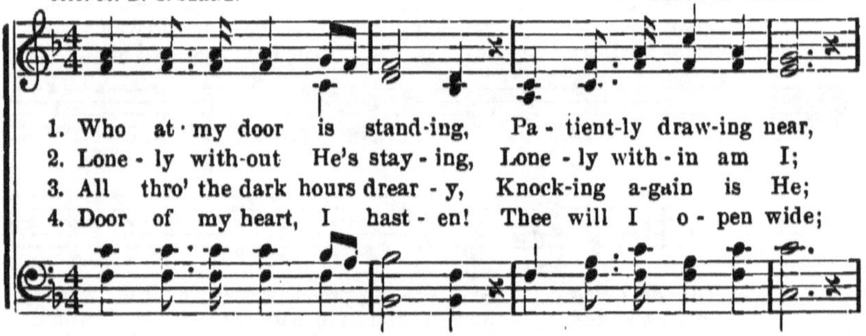

1. Who at my door is stand-ing, Pa - tient-ly draw-ing near,
2. Lone - ly with-out He's stay-ing, Lone - ly with - in am I;
3. All thro' the dark hours drear - y, Knock-ing a-gain is He;
4. Door of my heart, I hast - en! Thee will I o - pen wide;

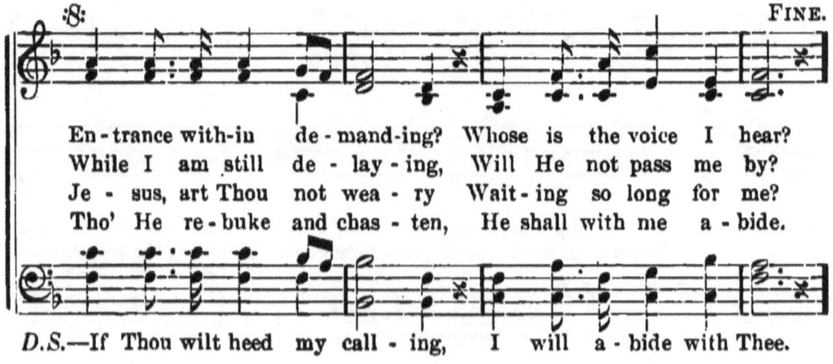

En - trance with-in de - mand-ing? Whose is the voice I hear?
While I am still de - lay - ing, Will He not pass me by?
Je - sus, art Thou not wea - ry Wait - ing so long for me?
Tho' He re - buke and chas - ten, He shall with me a - bide.

D.S.—If Thou wilt heed my call - ing, I will a - bide with Thee.

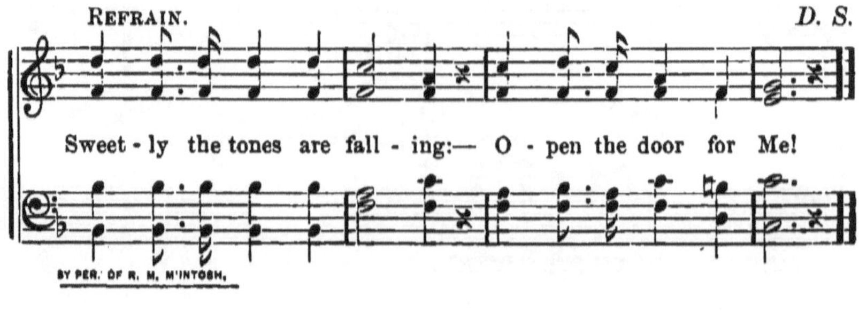

REFRAIN.   D. S.

Sweet - ly the tones are fall - ing:— O - pen the door for Me!

BY PER. OF R. M. M'INTOSH.

Rock of Ages.

Rit.

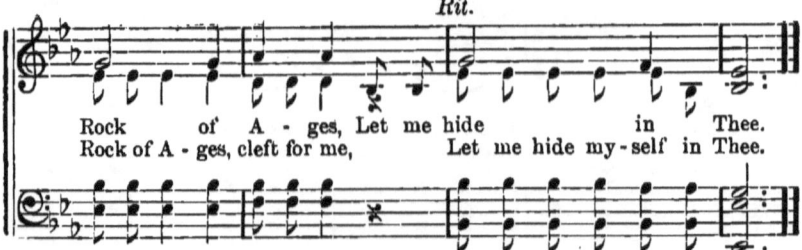

No. 200.   WHEN THE MIGHTY TRUMP.

Isaac Naylor.   For this Work.

1. The thun-ders of judg-ment shall crash through the skies,
   The dead, small and great, from their graves shall a-rise.
2. The cry shall be heard that the Bride-groom hath come
   To take His blest Bride to His own sa-cred home.
3. On the morn-ing of judg-ment, oh, where will you stand?
   On the left of the Shepherd, or at His right hand?
4. The lost one, in an-guish and sor-row and dread,
   Shall call for the mountains to fall on his head!

ff Chorus.

When the might-y, might-y, might-y trump Sounds, "Come, come a-way!" Oh, may we be read-y To hail that great day.

COPYRIGHT, 1894, BY CHAS. H. GABRIEL.

5 In robes of bright glory the saints shall be led
   Through heav'n's shining portals with Christ at their head!

6 The cherubs and seraphs and angels shall sing,
   And join with the ransomed in crowning their King!

7 Their voices in chorus like thunders shall rise,
   In crowning our Savior beyond the fair skies.

8 O sinner, don't linger! to Jesus repair;
   Make ready for death, and for judgment prepare!

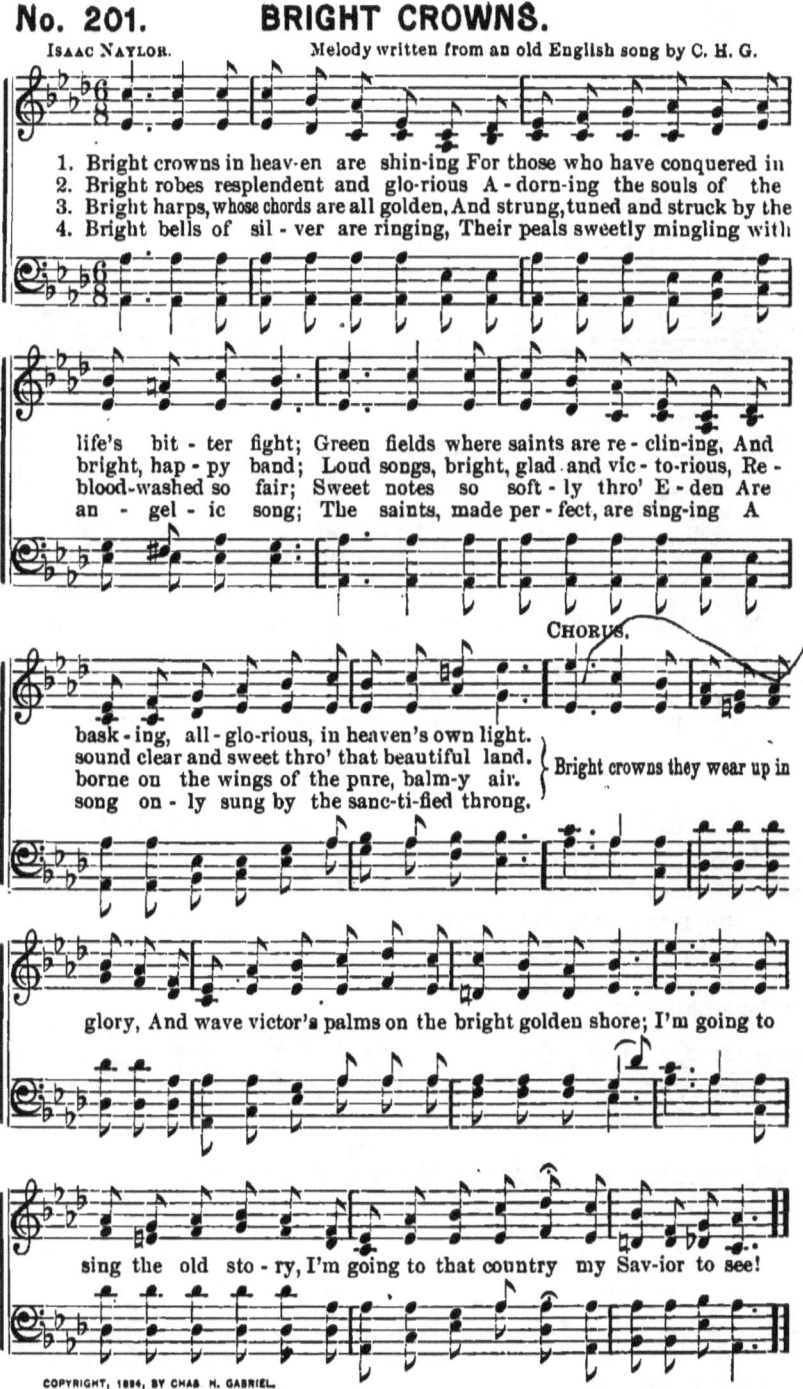

No. 202. BEAUTIFUL HOUR.

Mrs. Phœbe Palmer.   Mrs. Joseph F. Knapp.

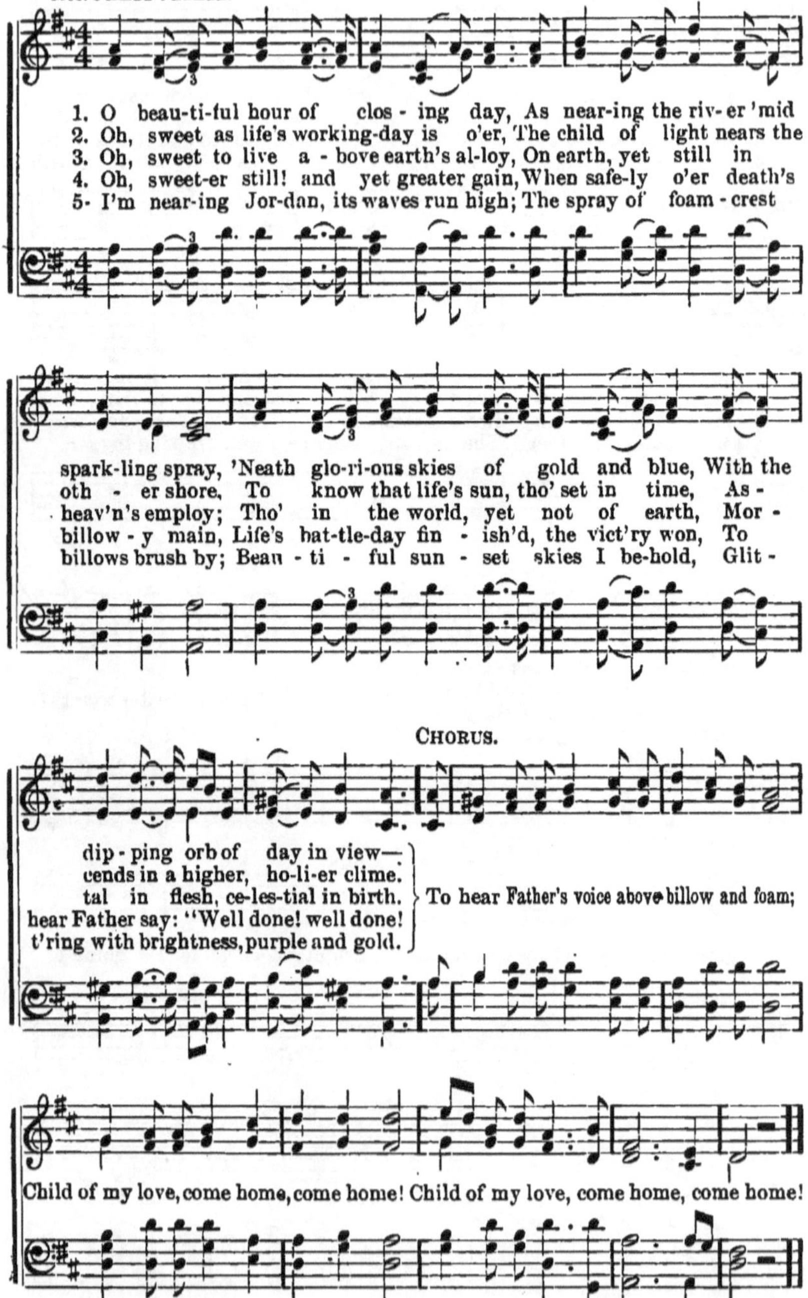

1. O beau-ti-ful hour of clos-ing day, As near-ing the riv-er 'mid
2. Oh, sweet as life's working-day is o'er, The child of light nears the
3. Oh, sweet to live a-bove earth's al-loy, On earth, yet still in
4. Oh, sweet-er still! and yet greater gain, When safe-ly o'er death's
5. I'm near-ing Jor-dan, its waves run high; The spray of foam-crest

spark-ling spray, 'Neath glo-ri-ous skies of gold and blue, With the
oth-er shore, To know that life's sun, tho' set in time, As-
heav'n's employ; Tho' in the world, yet not of earth, Mor-
billow-y main, Life's bat-tle-day fin-ish'd, the vict'ry won, To
billows brush by; Beau-ti-ful sun-set skies I be-hold, Glit-

Chorus.

dip-ping orb of day in view—
cends in a higher, ho-li-er clime.
tal in flesh, ce-les-tial in birth. } To hear Father's voice above billow and foam;
hear Father say: "Well done! well done!
t'ring with brightness, purple and gold.

Child of my love, come home, come home! Child of my love, come home, come home!

Copyright by Joseph F. Knapp.

No. 208. IN A LITTLE WHILE.

Rev. John Parker.   C. H. G.

1. We shall see the King, in a little while, 'Mid the splendor of His throne;
2. We shall see the Lamb as but newly slain, A-dor'd by the ransomed throng;
3. Our years on earth have been years of hope; Of the heav'n un-known we've craved;
4. In the lov-ing life in our Father's house, And the jas-per cit-y of gold,

Cho.—In a lit-tle while, just a lit-tle while, We shall know as we are known;

In the cit-y fair—we shall soon be there, Acknowledged and crowned His own.
In realms of light, and in robes of white, Shall join in the rapturous song.
But in boundless bliss, may our heav'n be this:—We shall share in the home of the saved.
No night is there, in its pal-ace fair, And its glo-ry can nev-er be told.

In a lit-tle while, just a little while, We shall meet and be crowned His own.

COPYRIGHT, 1894, BY CHAS. H. GABRIEL.

No. 209. THE CLEANSING WAVE.

Mrs. Phœbe Palmer.   Mrs. Jos. F. Knapp.

1. Oh, now I see the crimson wave, The fountain deep and wide Je-
2. I rise to walk in heav'n's own light, Above the world and sin, With
3. A-maz-ing grace! 'tis heav'n below To feel the blood ap-plied; And

CHORUS.

sus, my Lord, mighty to save, Points to His wounded side. } The cleansing stream
heart made pure, and garments white, And Christ enthron'd within. } Oh, praise the Lord!
Je-sus, on-ly Je-sus know, My Je-sus cru-ci-fied.

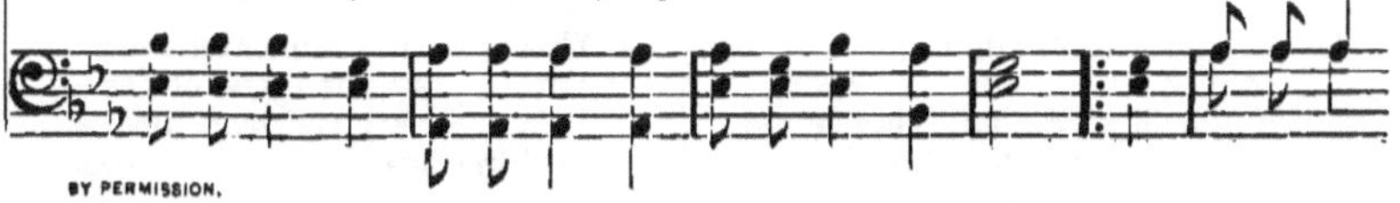

BY PERMISSION.

The Cleansing Wave.

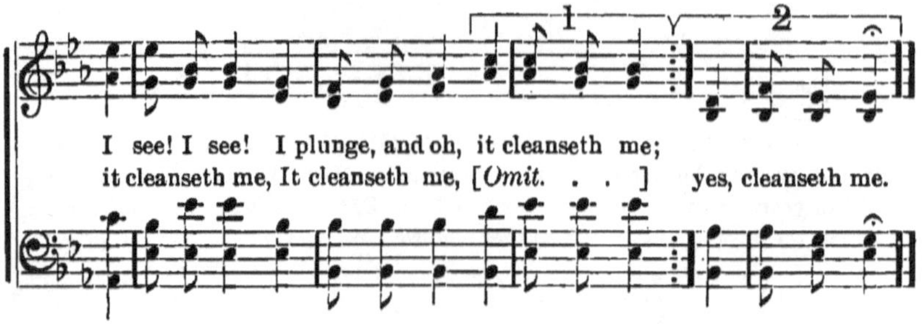

I see! I see! I plunge, and oh, it cleanseth me;
it cleanseth me, It cleanseth me, [*Omit* . . .] yes, cleanseth me.

No. 210. NOTHING BUT THE BLOOD OF JESUS.

R. L.   Robert Lowry.

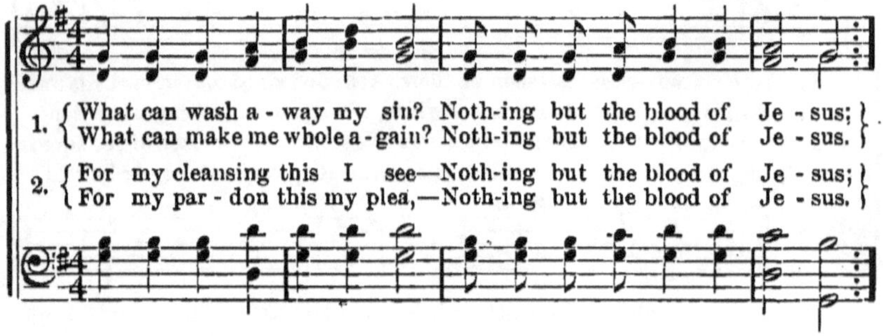

1. { What can wash a-way my sin? Noth-ing but the blood of Je-sus;
    What can make me whole a-gain? Noth-ing but the blood of Je-sus. }

2. { For my cleansing this I see—Noth-ing but the blood of Je-sus;
    For my par-don this my plea,—Noth-ing but the blood of Je-sus. }

CHORUS.

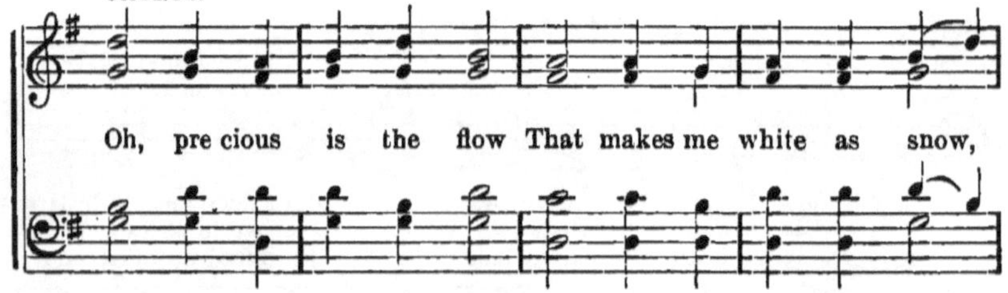

Oh, precious is the flow That makes me white as snow,
No oth-er Fount I know, Noth-ing but the Blood of Je-sus.

3 Nothing can for sin atone,
   Nothing but the blood of Jesus;
   Naught of good that I have done,
   Nothing but the blood of Jesus.

4 This is all my hope and peace—
   Nothing but the blood of Jesus;
   This is all my righteousness—
   Nothing but the blood of Jesus.

COPYRIGHT, 1876, BY ROBERT LOWRY.

No. 211. THE WAY OF THE CROSS.

Arr.

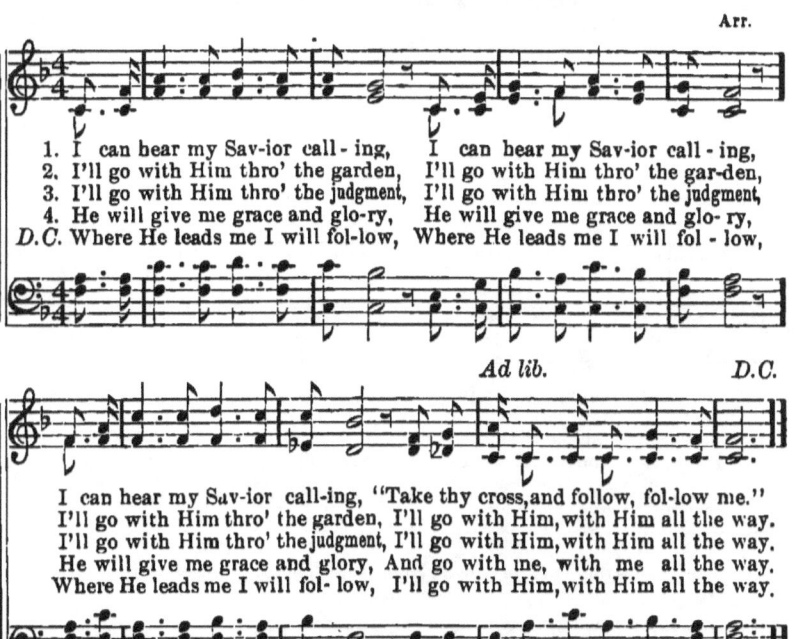

1. I can hear my Sav-ior call-ing, I can hear my Sav-ior call-ing,
2. I'll go with Him thro' the garden, I'll go with Him thro' the gar-den,
3. I'll go with Him thro' the judgment, I'll go with Him thro' the judgment,
4. He will give me grace and glo-ry, He will give me grace and glo-ry,
D.C. Where He leads me I will fol-low, Where He leads me I will fol-low,

Ad lib.   D.C.

I can hear my Sav-ior call-ing, "Take thy cross, and follow, fol-low me."
I'll go with Him thro' the garden, I'll go with Him, with Him all the way.
I'll go with Him thro' the judgment, I'll go with Him, with Him all the way.
He will give me grace and glory, And go with me, with me all the way.
Where He leads me I will fol-low, I'll go with Him, with Him all the way.

No. 212. MERIBAH.
Key of E♭.

1 Thou great mysterious God unknown,
Whose love hath gently led me on
E'en from my infant days;
Mine inmost soul expose to view,
And tell me if I ever knew
 Thy justifying grace.

2 If I have only known Thy fear,
And followed with a heart sincere,
 Thy drawings from above;
Now, now the further grace bestow,
And let my sprinkled conscience know
 Thy sweet forgiving love.

3 Short of Thy love I would not stop,
A stranger to the gospel hope,
 The sense of sin forgiven;
I would not, Lord, my soul deceive,
Without the inward witness live,
 That antepast of heaven.

4 If now the witness were in me,
Would he not testify of Thee,
 In Jesus reconciled?
And should I not with faith draw nigh,
And boldly, "Abba, Father," cry,
 And know myself Thy child?

213. REGENT SQUARE.
Key of B♭.

1 O thou God of my salvation,
 My Redeemer from all sin;
Moved by Thy divine compassion,
 Who hast died my heart to win,
  I will praise thee;
 Where shall I Thy praise begin?

2 Though unseen, I love the Savior;
 He hath brought salvation near;
Manifests His pardoning favor;
 And when Jesus doth appear,
  Soul and body
 Shall his glorious image bear.

3 While the angel choirs are crying,
 "Glory to the great I AM,"
I with them will still be vying—
 Glory! glory to the Lamb!
  O how precious
 Is the sound of Jesus' name!

4 Angels now are hovering round us,
 Unperceived amid the throng;
Wondering at the love that crowned us,
 Glad to join the holy song:
  Hallelujah,
 Love and praise to Christ belong!

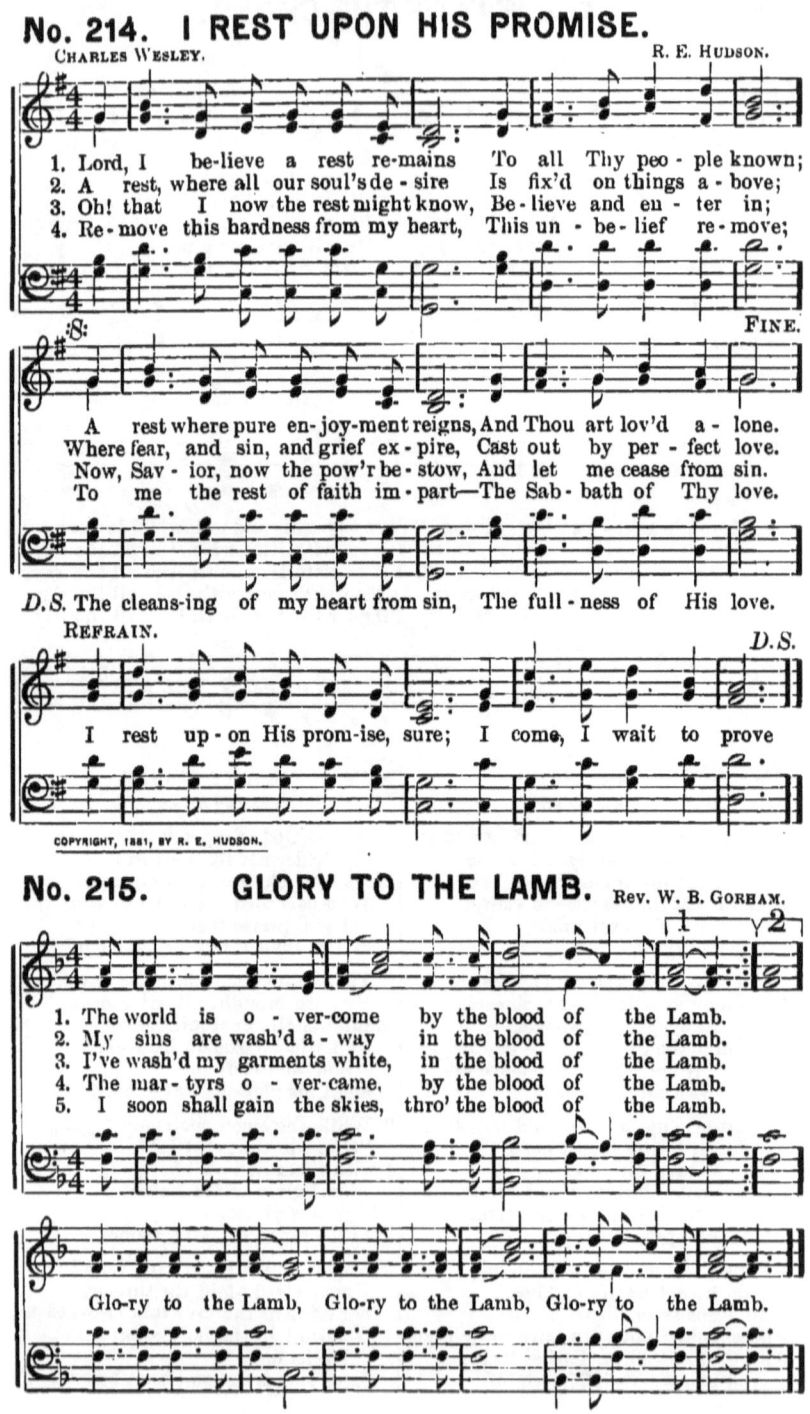

No. 216. WE ARE PASSING AWAY.

J. HART. Arr. by W. J. K.

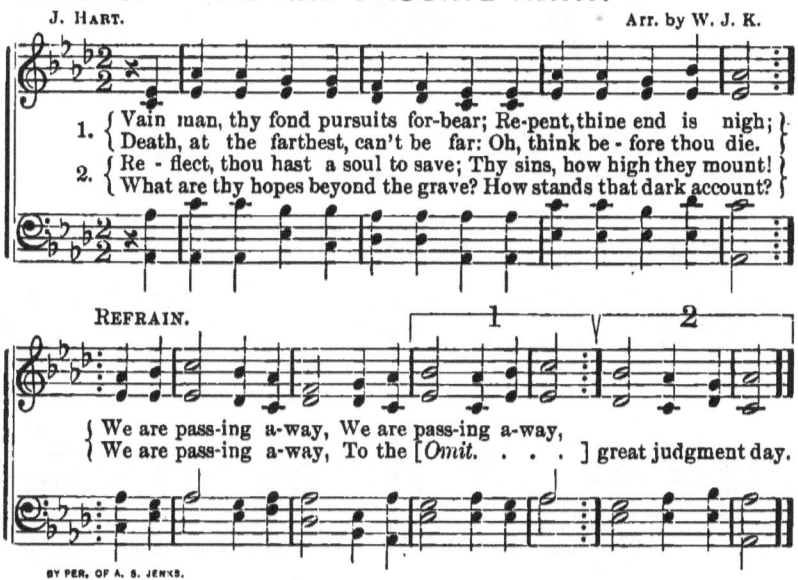

1. Vain man, thy fond pursuits for-bear; Re-pent, thine end is nigh;
   Death, at the farthest, can't be far: Oh, think be-fore thou die.
2. Re - flect, thou hast a soul to save; Thy sins, how high they mount!
   What are thy hopes beyond the grave? How stands that dark account?

REFRAIN.

We are pass-ing a-way, We are pass-ing a-way,
We are pass-ing a-way, To the [Omit. . . .] great judgment day.

BY PER. OF A. S. JENKS.

3 Death enters, and there's no defence;
  His time there's none can tell;
  He'll in a moment call thee hence,
  To heaven, or down to hell.

4 Thy flesh, perhaps thy greatest care,
  Shall into dust consume;
  But, ah! destruction ends not there;
  Sin kills beyond the tomb.

No. 217. JESUS, HIDE ME.

FRED. WOODROW. C. H. G.

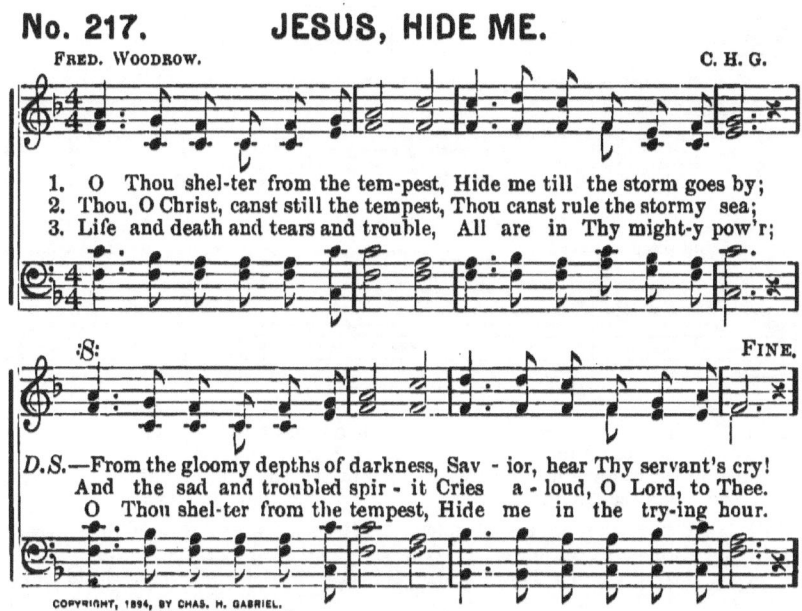

1. O Thou shel-ter from the tem-pest, Hide me till the storm goes by;
2. Thou, O Christ, canst still the tempest, Thou canst rule the stormy sea;
3. Life and death and tears and trouble, All are in Thy might-y pow'r;

FINE.

D.S.—From the gloomy depths of darkness, Sav - ior, hear Thy servant's cry!
And the sad and troubled spir - it Cries a - loud, O Lord, to Thee.
O Thou shel-ter from the tempest, Hide me in the try-ing hour.

COPYRIGHT, 1894, BY CHAS. H. GABRIEL.

Jesus, Hide Me.

REFRAIN. D. S.

Je-sus, hide me, Je-sus, hide me, Hide me till the storm goes by;

No. 218. EXHORTATION.

1. Je-sus, Thine all - vic-to - rious love Shed in my heart a-broad;
Then shall my feet no long-er rove, Root-ed and fixed in God..........
Then shall my feet no long-er rove,

2 Oh, that in me the sacred fire
Might now begin to glow;
Burn up the dross of base desire,
And make the mountains flow.

3 Oh, that it now from heav'n might [fall,
And all my sins consume;
Come, Holy Ghost, for Thee I call;
Spirit of burning, come.

4 Refining fire, go through my heart;
Illuminate my soul;
Scatter Thy life through every part,
And sanctify the whole.

5 My steadfast soul, from falling free,
Shall then no longer move,
While Christ is all the world to me,
And all my heart is love.

No. 219. PURER IN HEART.

J. H. Fillmore.

1. Pur-er in heart, O God, Help me to be; May I devote my life Wholly to Thee. Watch Thou my wayward feet, Guide me with counsel sweet; Pur-er in heart, Help me to be.
2. Pur-er in heart, O God, Help me to be; Teach me to do Thy will Most lovingly. Be Thou my Friend and Guide, Let me with Thee abide; Pur-er in heart, Help me to be.
3. Pur-er in heart, O God, Help me to be; That I Thy holy face One day may see. Keep me from secret sin, Reign Thou my soul within Pur-er in heart, Help me to be.

COPYRIGHT, BY FILLMORE BROS.

No. 220. STEP OUT ON THE PROMISE.

Maggie Potter. Arr. by E. F. M.   E. F. Miller.

1. O mourn-er in Zi-on, how bless-ed art thou, For Je-sus is
2. O ye that are hun-gry and thirst-y, re-joice! For ye shall be
3. Who sighs for a heart from in-i-qui-ty free? Oh, poor, troubled
4. Step out on the promise, And Christ you shall win, "The blood of His

BY PERMISSION.

Step Out on the Promise.

wait-ing to com-fort thee now, Fear not to re-ly on the
filled; do you hear that sweet voice In-vit-ing you now to the
soul! there's a prom-ise for thee, There's rest, wea-ry one, in the
Son cleans-eth us from all sin," It cleans-eth me now, hal-le-

word of thy God; Step out on the prom-ise,—get un-der the blood.
ban-quet of God? Step out on the prom-ise,—get un-der the blood.
bo-som of God; Step out on the prom-ise,—get un-der the blood.
lu-jah to God! I rest on His prom-ise,—I'm un-der the blood.

No. 221. CHRIST IS PRECIOUS.

ELIZA SHERMAN.   J. H. FILLMORE.

1. O the pre-cious love of Je-sus, Growing sweeter day by day,
Tun-ing all my heart so joy-ous To a heav'nly mel-o-dy.

CHORUS.

Christ is precious, Christ is precious, In life's journey He will lead thee;
Christ is precious, Christ is precious, He will lead thee all the [*Omit.*] way.

COPYRIGHT BY FILLMORE BROS.

2 But we cannot know the fullness
   Of the Savior's wondrous love,
   Till we see and know His glory,
   In the heav'nly home above.

3 Come and taste the love of Jesus,
   At His feet thy burdens lay;
   Trust Him with thy grief and sorrow,
   Bear this joyful song away.

No. 222. THOU THINKEST, LORD, OF ME.

E. D. Mund.
E. S. Lorenz.

1. A-mid the tri-als which I meet, Amid the thorns that pierce my feet,
2. The cares of life come thronging fast, Up-on my soul their shadow cast;
3. Let shadows come, let shadows go, Let life be bright or dark with woe,

One thought remains su-preme-ly sweet, Thou thinkest, Lord, of me!
Their gloom reminds my heart at last, Thou thinkest, Lord, of me!
I am con-tent for this I know, Thou thinkest, Lord, of me!

D.S.—What need I fear since Thou art near, And think-est, Lord, of me.

CHORUS.   D.S.

Thou think-est, Lord, of me, Thou thinkest, Lord, of me.
of me, of me.

BY PERMISSION.

No. 223. SATISFIED.

Clara Teare.
R. E. Hudson.

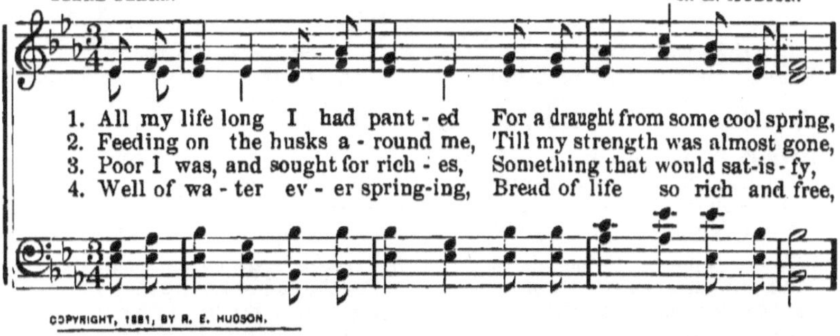

1. All my life long I had pant-ed For a draught from some cool spring,
2. Feeding on the husks a-round me, 'Till my strength was almost gone,
3. Poor I was, and sought for rich-es, Something that would sat-is-fy,
4. Well of wa-ter ev-er spring-ing, Bread of life so rich and free,

COPYRIGHT, 1881, BY R. E. HUDSON.

Satisfied.

That I hop'd would quench the burning Of the thirst I felt with-in.
Long'd my soul for something bet-ter, On-ly still to hun-ger on.
But the dust I gather'd round me, On-ly mock'd my soul's sad cry.
Un-told wealth that nev-er fail-eth, My Re-deem-er is to me.

REFRAIN.
Hal-le-lu-jah! I have found it—What my soul so long has craved!
Je-sus sat-is-fies my longings; Thro' His blood I now am saved.

No. 224. SWEET BY AND BY.
Key of G.

1 There's a land that is fairer than day,
   And by faith we can see it afar,
For the Father waits over the way,
   To prepare us a dwelling-place there.

CHORUS.
In the sweet by and by
We shall meet on that beautiful shore,
   In the sweet by and by
We shall meet on that beautiful shore.

2 We shall sing on that beautiful shore
   The melodious songs of the blest,
And our spirits shall sorrow no more,
   Not a sigh for the blessing of rest.

3 To our bountiful Father above
   We will offer the tribute of praise,
For the glorious gift of His love
   And the blessings that hallow our days.

No. 225. OVER THERE.
Key of A.

1 Oh, think of a home over there,
   By the side of the river of light,
Where the saints, all immortal and fair,
   Are robed in their garments of white.

CHORUS.
Over there, over there,
Oh, think of a home over there,
   Over there, over there,
Oh, think of a home over there.

2 Oh, think of the friends over there,
   Who before us the journey have trod;
Of the songs that they breathe on the air
   In their home in the palace of God.

3 I'll soon be at home over there,
   For the end of my journey I see;
Many dear to my heart over there,
   Are watching and waiting for me.

No. 226. **JESUS SAVES ME.**

C. H. G.

1. I have no mer-it of my own, My on-ly plea is Je-sus!
   I'm saved by Him and Him a-lone, My on-ly plea is Je-sus!
2. He is the Truth, the Life, the Way, My on-ly plea is Je-sus!
   It fills my soul with joy to say, My on-ly plea is Je-sus!
3. When in the Judgment I shall stand, My on-ly plea is Je-sus!
   I shall be safe at God's right hand, My on-ly plea is Je-sus!

CHORUS.

Je - sus saves me, Je-sus saves me ev-'ry day, I am hap-py on my homeward way! Yes, Je - sus saves me ev-'ry day, Glo-ry to His name!

COPYRIGHT, 1894 BY CHAS. H GABRIEL.

No. 227. LENOX.

Key of B♭.

1 Arise, my soul, arise;
  Shake off thy guilty fears,
The bleeding Sacrifice
  In my behalf appears:
Before the throne my Surety stands,
My name is written on His hands

2 He ever lives above,
  For me to intercede;
His all-redeeming love,
  His precious blood, to plead;
His blood atoned for all our race,
And sprinkles now the throne of grace.

3 Five bleeding wounds He bears,
  Received on Calvary:
They pour effectual prayers,
  They strongly plead for me,
"Forgive him, O, forgive," they cry,
"Nor let that ransomed sinner die."

No. 228. ZION.

Key of D.

1 On the mountain's top appearing,
  Lo! the sacred herald stands,
Welcome news to Zion bearing,
  Zion, long in hostile lands:
    Mourning captive!
God Himself shall loose thy bands.

2 Has thy night been long and mournful?
  Have thy friends unfaithful proved?
Have thy foes been proud and scornful,
  By thy sighs and tears unmoved?
    Cease thy mourning;
Zion still is well beloved.

3 Peace and joy shall now attend thee;
  All thy warfare now is past;
God thy Savior will defend thee;
  Victory is thine at last:
    All thy conflicts
End in everlasting rest.

No. 229. HE IS CALLING.

F. W. Faber.

1. There's a wideness in God's mercy, Like the wideness of the sea;
   There's a kindness in His justice Which is more than [*Omit.*] lib-er-ty.
2. There is wel-come for the sinner, And more graces for the good;
   There is mer-cy with the Savior, There is heal-ing [*Omit.*] in His blood.

CHORUS.

He is call-ing, "Come to me!" Lord, I glad-ly haste to Thee.

3 For the love of God is broader
  Than the measure of man's mind;
  And the heart of the Eternal
  Is most wonderfully kind.

4 If our love were but more simple,
  We should take Him at His word;
  And our lives would be all sunshine
  In the sweetness of our Lord.

No. 230. HOLY SPIRIT, FAITHFUL GUIDE.

M. M. W.
M. M. Wells.

FINE.

1. Ho-ly Spir-it, faith-ful guide, Ev-er near the Christian's side;
   Gent-ly lead us by the hand, Pil-grims in a des-ert land;
2. Ev-er pres-ent, tru-est Friend, Ev-er near Thine aid to lend;
   Leave us not to doubt and fear, Grop-ing on in dark-ness drear;
3. When our days of toil shall cease, Wait-ing still for sweet re-lease,
   Noth-ing left but heav'n and pray'r, Wond'ring if our names are there;

D.C.—Whisper soft-ly, "wand'rer come! Fol-low me, I'll guide thee home."

D.C.

Wea-ry souls for-e'er re-joice, While they hear that sweet-est voice,
When the storms are rag-ing sore, Hearts grow faint, and hopes give o'er,
Wad-ing deep the dis-mal flood, Plead-ing naught but Je-sus' blood,

INDEX.

TITLES IN SMALL CAPS, FIRST LINES IN ROMAN.

A Fountain of Life	88	Called to the feast	67
AFTERWARD	22	CAN IT BE	171
A GREAT GLAD DAY	185	CHRIST, AND CHRIST ALONE	193
Alas, and did my	21, 42	Christ is my Savior	169
ALL FOR THEE	122	CHRIST IS PRECIOUS	221
ALL HAIL THE POWER	102	Christ of all my hopes	93
All hail the power of	102, 160	CLINGING TO THE CROSS	75
All my life long	223	COME, BRETHREN DEAR	177
All the way my Lord	1	Come, follow in the	107
ALL THINGS ARE POSSIBLE	112	COME INTO THE FOLD	11
AMERICA	113	Come, let us join our	7
Am I a Soldier of	26	Come, my fond fluttering	204
Amid the trials	222	COME, THOU FOUNT	37
ANYWHERE WITH JESUS	27	COME TO JESUS	109
A PERFECT HEART	59	Come, ye sinners	105
Are you peaceful in	187	COMING THIS WAY	135
Arise, my Soul, Arise	227	CORONATION	160
ARE YOU WALKING IN THE	60	CORNET	205
A SHELTER IN THE TIME	45	Cross and Crown	69
ASLEEP IN JESUS	154		
AT THE CROSS	42	DARE TO DO RIGHT	139
AT THE LANDING	49	Dare to think, though	139
		DENNIS	143
BEAUTIFUL HOUR	202	DEPTH OF MERCY	94
BE A GOLDEN SUNBEAM	2	Does the thought ever	140
BEAR THE TORCH OF THE LORD	77	Do life's cares and	18
BECAUSE HE LOVED US SO	125	Down at the Cross	172
BEHOLD ME STANDING AT	127		
BENEATH HIS WING	15	EXHORTATION	218
BENEATH THE SHADE OF	71		
Beyond the ills that	185	FAITH TRIUMPHANT	13
BLESSED ASSURANCE	35	Fierce is the tempest	75
BLESSED JESUS	166	FOOTSTEPS OF JESUS	107
BLESSED REDEEMER GREAT	64	Forever with the Lord	168
Blest be the tie	143	For the sighing and	33
BLIND BARTIMEUS	28	Forward be our	138
BRIGHT CROWNS	201	FORWARD INTO LIGHT	138
BRING THEM TO JESUS	18	FOUNTAIN OF LIFE	88
BRINGING IN THE SHEAVES	145	From Egypt's cruel	76
BY AND BY	17	FULL CONSECRATION	204

GATHERING THE HARVEST	110	I'll praise Thee Savior	23
GENTLY LEAD US	147	I LONG TO BEHOLD HIM	48
GLAD TIDINGS	30	I'M ALWAYS SAFE WITH	181
GLORIA PATRI	233	IN A LITTLE WHILE	208
GLORY TO HIS NAME	172	In a world where	115
GLORY TO THE LAMB	38, 215	In from the highways	144
GOD CALLING YET	50	In evil long I took	62
Go spread the joyful	118	IN THE BY AND BY	189
Guide me, O Thou	98	In the dawning of	84
		In the morn of morns	151
Hail to the brightness	146	IN THE SHADOW OF THE	3
HAPPY DAY	182	In yon land of light	17
HALLELUJAH	51	I REST UPON HIS PROMISE	214
Hark! salvation's notes	203	ISHI	194
Hark! sinner, list	159	IT WILL NEVER GROW OLD	183
Hark! the notes of	38	I've a message from	8
HAVE MERCY	21	I've looked my life over	100
Have you heard, O	108	I was a wandering	191
HAVE YOU LEARNED TO PRAY	106		
HEAR THE SAVIOR CALLING	116	Jesus, and shall it ever	68
HEAVENLY REST	168	JESUS, HIDE ME	217
HE HAS COME	190	Jesus, I my cross have	92
HE HATH REDEEMED ME	169	Jesus, my all to	111
HE IS ABLE TO DELIVER	142	Jesus, my Lord, to	117
HE IS CALLING	229	JESUS ONLY	70
HE IS COMING AGAIN	176	JESUS SAVES ME	226
HE LEADETH ME	80	JESUS, THE LIFE-BOAT	100
HE LEADS AND GUIDES ME	74	Jesus, Thine all-victorious	218
HE LEAVES IT ALL WITH THEE	97	JESUS WILL BE YOURS	35
HE LOVES THEM	165	JOY AMONG THE ANGELS	173
HE REDEEMED ME	32	JUST AS I AM	41
HE SAVES ME TO-DAY	111	JUST BEYOND THE RIVER	19
HIS LOVE	118		
Holy Spirit, faithful	230	Keep me near to Thee	91
HOME, SWEET HOME	133	KING OF KINGS AND LORD	96
HOW WILL YOU DO	120		
		LEAD ME	95
I am coming for	75	LEAD ME, SAVIOR	46
I am coming to the cross	188	Lead me, dear Savior	95
I am saved in the	56	LEAVE IT TO HIM	43
I am so glad that	161	LET HIM IN	184
I AM THE WAY	144	Let mountains and	73
I am trusting in the	101	LET NOT YOUR HEART BE	40
I am trusting Jesus	70	LET THE SAVIOR IN	196
I AM TRUSTING, LORD, IN THEE	188	Like Jacob in his	207
I AM TRUSTING THEE	44	LIVING IN CANAAN	7
I am walking with	83	Long ago the Savior	193
I believe that Jesus	13	LOOK AND LIVE	8
I can hear my Savior	211	Look, look, the foe	36
I do not know the pathway	181	Lord, I believe a rest	214
I FEEL LIKE TRAVELLING ON	63	Lord, my heart is rested	121
If my poor name is	90		
If on a quiet sea	123	MARCHING TO THE LAND ABOVE	124
If you come to Jesus	35	MARCHING TO ZION	26
If you want pardon	71	'Mid scenes of confusion	133
I have found redemption	87	MOMENT BY MOMENT	57
I have no merit in	226	MORE LOVE TO THEE	174
I hear them sing of	171	Must Jesus bear the	69
I know that my Redeemer	72	My country, 'tis of thee	113
I'LL LIVE FOR HIM	31	My faith looks up	99
		My heavenly home is	63

www.ingramcontent.com/pod-product-compliance
Lightning Source LLC
Chambersburg PA
CBHW031817230426
43669CB00009B/1174